101 *Glimpses of Historic* Micanopy

101 *Glimpses of Historic* Micanopy

STEVE RAJTAR

THE History PRESS

Published by The History Press
Charleston, SC 29403
www.historypress.net

First published 2008

Manufactured in the United States

ISBN 978.1.59629.509.4

Library of Congress Cataloging-in-Publication Data
Rajtar, Steve, 1951-
101 glimpses of historic Micanopy / Steve Rajtar.
p. cm.
Includes bibliographical references.
ISBN 978-1-59629-509-4
1. Micanopy (Fla.)--History--Pictorial works. 2. Micanopy (Fla.)--Social life and customs--Pictorial works. 3. Historic buildings--Florida--Micanopy--Pictorial works. 4. Micanopy (Fla.)--Buildings, structures, etc.--Pictorial works. I. Title. II. Title: One hundred one glimpses of historic Micanopy. III. Title: One hundred and one glimpses of historic Micanopy.
F319.M64R35 2008
975.9'79--dc22
2008019745

Contents

Preface

Micanopy was one of the earliest Florida towns, and it could have followed the same route as others, evolving into a modern city with high-tech, glitzy tourist attractions. Other locales in Florida did just that and are now home to T-shirt shops, theme restaurants and other eye-catching, dollar-attracting exhibits and rides. Like those locales, Micanopy moved from a center of commerce and agriculture to today's tourist attraction—but not the type that uses bright lights and audio-animatronics.

Instead, Micanopy attracts those seeking a quiet day searching for just the right piece of art or antique collectible. The stores and restaurants are as unique as the items they offer. There are no franchises, no chains and no store logos recognizable outside of the town limits. What you find in Micanopy are friendly shopkeepers who would love to engage you in a conversation about pretty much anything while helping you to find that particular literary or antique treasure that you would never find in a chain store or mall.

This town, located off the highway between Gainesville and Ocala, in many ways hasn't yet caught up with the twenty-first century, or for that matter, most of the twentieth century. For some sites, you can't tell if a photo was taken yesterday or fifty years ago. When you visit Micanopy, you're welcomed back to a simpler time. Hopefully, it will always be that way.

A Brief History of Micanopy

When Hernando de Soto arrived in the area on August 12, 1539, with 620 soldiers and 223 horses, the place now called Micanopy was the site of a Potano Indian village. Likely, de Soto stayed for a short time, enslaved a few natives and forced them to carry part of the village's food supply northward on the conquistador's search for gold.

During the late 1640s, the nearby Paynes Prairie area was turned into a large cattle ranch by Don Francisco Menéndez Marqués. He soon died of yellow fever in his home city of St. Augustine, and the ranch was continued by his family. The Potano natives provided cheap labor for the Spanish owners and overseers. The natives revolted in 1656, and in the eight months of fighting, many of the cattle were killed. Those that survived roamed freely and formed the basis for Florida's cattle industry in later years.

Thomas Menéndez Marqués moved to Paynes Prairie in about 1670 and revived the cattle ranch. He called it *La Chua*, based on a Potano word for "jug." The name came from the

Alachua Sink on the north edge of the prairie, often referred to as the "big jug," which filled and emptied over time.

Creek Indians from Georgia in the early 1700s supported the British in their conflicts with the Spanish. In 1704, the Creeks attacked the La Chua ranch and reduced it in size, although it was able to continue supplying some meat to the soldiers at the Castillo de San Marcos in St. Augustine. With the aid of the British, the Creeks set out to eliminate the Potanos and other Timucuans in the area, and the Creek presence caused the Spanish government to shut down the La Chua ranch for good in 1706.

By the 1730s, the Creeks dominated the region, which by that time was essentially abandoned by the Spanish. In about 1750, the Oconee Creeks, led by Chief Cowkeeper, moved to the south edge of Paynes Prairie, and it is believed that they took over the former village site of the Potanos. Not long afterward, the drain for the sinkhole on the prairie became plugged and the area turned into what became known as Alachua Lake. It became a good place to fish until, about fifteen years later, the lake dried up and the rotting fish smell caused the Oconees to move away and establish a new village site.

The Oconees moved to the northwest shore of Lake Tuscawilla, the present site of the town of Micanopy. They called their village *Cuscowilla*, and Cowkeeper personally told the governor of Georgia that his goal was to kill Spaniards and any natives who allied with them. Other groups of Creeks came to Florida and allied with the British, but Cowkeeper maintained his tribe's independence from other native groups. As a result, they acquired the name of *semanolies*, meaning "wild men" or "runaways," and soon became known as the Seminoles.

Naturalist William Bartram visited the Seminole town in 1774 and found about thirty residences. He documented many species of plants and animals, including the now-extinct Florida red wolf. Although he described the Seminole village in great detail, no one is sure today precisely where it was located. It is generally agreed that it was situated somewhere within the town limits of today's Micanopy.

In about 1790, Cowkeeper died and was succeeded by his son, King Payne, for whom the nearby prairie is named. He moved the Seminoles (then called the Alachua Seminoles to distinguish them from other former Creeks throughout the state) a little to the east, to the new settlement of Paynestown. In 1812, the U.S. Army, led by Colonel Daniel Newnan, engaged the Seminoles in battle as they were leaving Paynestown on an expedition to St. Augustine. As a result, the Alachua Seminoles abandoned Paynestown and left the area.

The white settlement of the area a little south of Gainesville, which we now know as Micanopy, began with the December 22, 1817 land grant made by Spain to Don Fernando de la Maza Arredondo, a merchant from Havana, Cuba. Called the Arredondo Grant, the land was a square twenty miles on a side and included Micanopy and Paynes Prairie.

Don Fernando was given the land as compensation for his efforts in 1811 in obtaining troops to protect the Spaniards in St. Augustine and in using his own funds to help the city in lean economic times. The grant was made on the condition that he had to settle at least two hundred families on the land within three years from the date of the grant. Don Fernando himself never resided on the land, but instead he intended to market tracts to others interested in establishing homes there.

The area in the late 1810s was inhabited by natives who could have been an impediment to settlement. It was less than five years following the end of the First Seminole War, and Arredondo feared that these natives would make it difficult to find two hundred willing families to satisfy the condition of the grant. He brought in Horatio S. Dexter to help smooth relations with the local natives, and Dexter brought in Edward M. Wanton, a trader who had lived for years with the natives.

A little to the north, Moses Levy acquired a hundred thousand acres that included a portion of the Arredondo Grant, and on it he established the Pilgrimage Plantation as a home for Jewish settlers. For a time, the plantation produced a crop of sugar cane. The area began to attract some settlement interest and Arredondo requested and received an eighteen-month extension on the requirement to settle two hundred families on his land. The first two settlers who

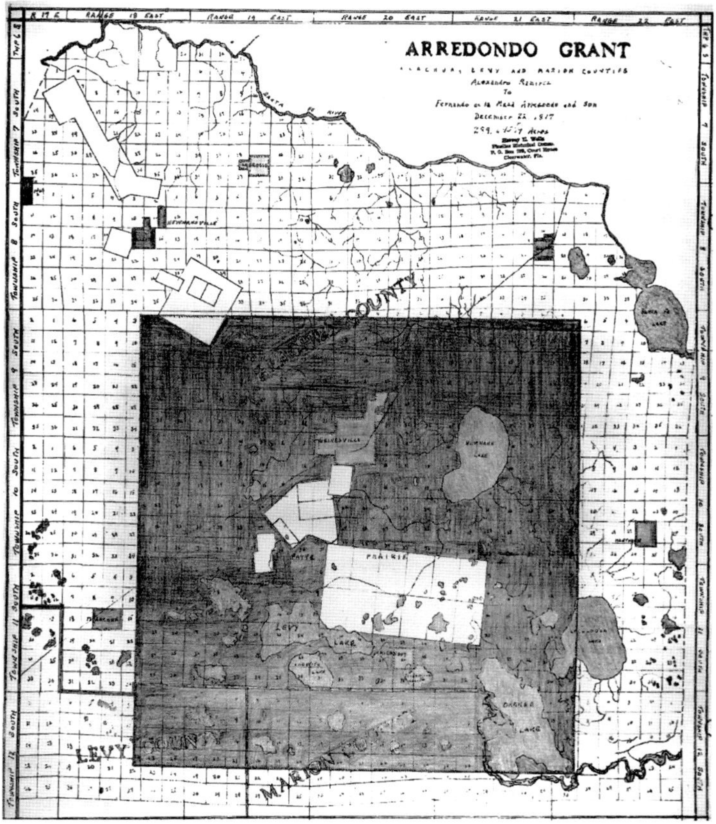

ARREDONDO MAP

Shown on this map are the 289,645 acres in three counties that constituted the Arredondo Grant. Micanopy is just south of the white rectangle. *Image courtesy of the Florida Photographic Collection.*

arrived were John Smith and Patrick Lannam, both of whom built log cabins near Lake Tuscawilla. Edward Wanton also built a combination house and store building.

Spain ceded Florida to the United States in 1821, with the condition that all Spanish land grants would be honored. A challenge was made to the validity of the Arredondo Grant for the reason that Don Fernando had only about twenty, and not two hundred, families living there. The Supreme Court, in its 1832 session, found that the condition had indeed not been strictly satisfied, but it was sufficiently impressed with Fernando's efforts and refused to take the land away from him. Don Fernando and the settlers who traced their titles back through him were allowed to keep their land, but further legal challenges did not clear up the last of their land title problems until 1850.

Edward Wanton called the settlement Micanopy after the Seminole chief who initially was friendly and cooperative. Others in the area wanted it called Wanton or Wantons, and the first post office bore that name. It served as a stopping point for travelers passing through Alachua County, a central crossroads between most of the major coastal towns. Some came by wagon via the Alachua Trail. Others traveled by water on the St. Johns River and Orange Lake.

Micanopy also appeared to have a future as a governmental center. Florida originally was two territories that merged into one in 1821. The initial capitals, St. Augustine and Pensacola, each wanted to be the capital of the single large Florida. Dr.

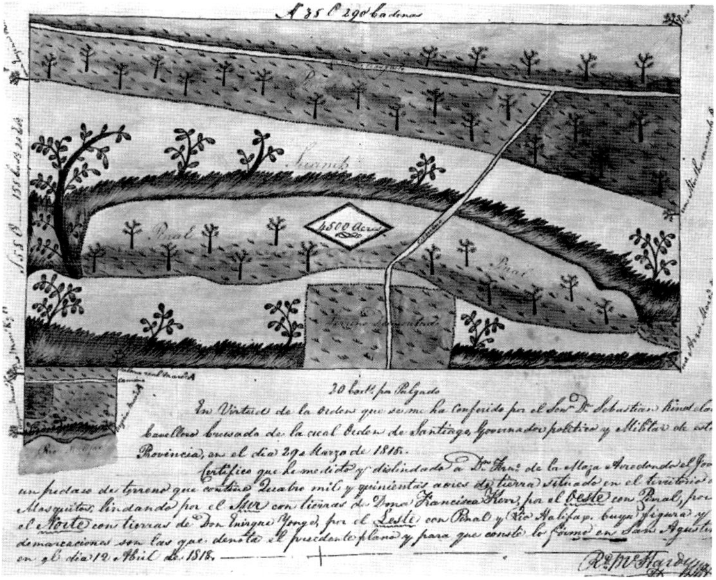

Arredondo Land Grant

This is the 1818 document granting land to Don Fernando de la Maza Arredondo. It is signed by Robert McHardy, a government-appointed surveyor. *Image courtesy of the Florida Photographic Collection.*

William Simmons of St. Augustine was enlisted to help locate an appropriate location for a capital, and he visited Micanopy in 1822. Simmons predicted that the settlement would eventually become the capital of Florida.

In 1823, Simmons was sent by the territorial governor, along with John Williams of Pensacola, with instructions

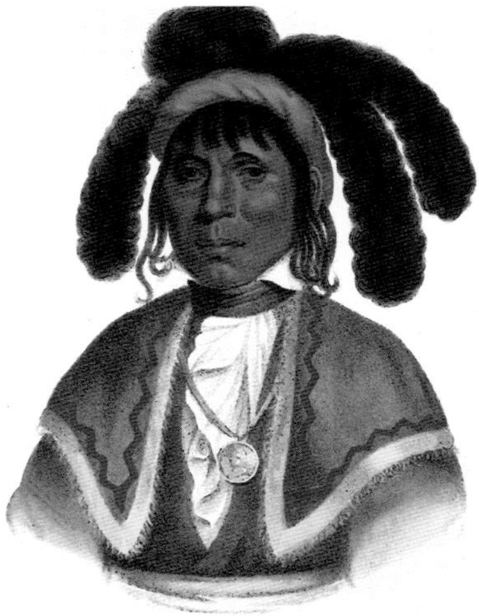

CHIEF MICANOPY
In 1812, soldiers attacked Cuscowilla and killed Chief Payne, who was succeeded by Chief Micanopy. The town was named for him in 1834. *Image courtesy of the Florida Photographic Collection.*

to select a capital site approximately midway between St. Augustine and Pensacola. Micanopy did not quite satisfy the geographic requirement, and they selected Tallahassee instead. Although Micanopy did not become the state capital, in 1824 it was named the temporary seat of the new Alachua County, which included land from the Georgia border southward almost to Tampa.

Wanton's trading post was the venue for all early important meetings in that part of Florida. It was where traveling circuit riders preached, including the well-known John L. Jerry and Isaac Boring. By 1826, the settlement included a post office, a sawmill and twenty-five homes. Nevertheless, the permanent county seat was established at Newnansville because it was located along the Bellamy Road that connected St. Augustine and Pensacola.

During the Second Seminole War of 1835–42, two forts operated near Lake Tuscawilla to protect settlers living on the south side of Paynes Prairie. The first was Fort Defiance, built in April 1835. Soldiers stationed there saw action in five battles, including the battle of Micanopy. That fort was burned by the army in 1836 in an effort to stop an outbreak of fever. It was rebuilt on the same site in April 1837 and given the name of Fort Micanopy. It consisted of corner blockhouses with picket work in between, and it formed a 250-foot square. It served as a military hospital and supply depot until its deactivation in 1843.

The late 1840s saw increased migration to the region, and land sales accelerated. In 1849, Joel B. Smith purchased the 640 acres that composed Micanopy, and he later sold off portions. Early Micanopy had several stores, and pioneers from the countryside came to town to shop. By 1850, John H. Zewadski had a store on the main street of Cholokka Avenue, between Ocala and Seminary Avenues. He had been an officer in the Polish army and was a political refugee, and Micanopy was a safe place to hide from the problems in his homeland. A few years later, on the same site, Drs. Cooper and Mathers opened their apothecary shop.

Later known as the Old Reliable Drug Store, their store also housed the post office, and Augustus Mathers served as the postmaster. The store served as the stop for the coaches of the Hart Stage Line, which began running in 1860 and carried both mail and passengers from the county seat of Newnansville along the western edge of Alachua Lake and entered Micanopy from the west.

Industry began in Micanopy in about 1850, when George Riggs and James Benneker started manufacturing wagons and carriages. By 1856, Colonel George Leitner was brought in as a partner and they modernized their factory. To upgrade their power source to run their machinery, they replaced the blind horse they had walking on a treadmill with a steam engine that produced twelve horsepower. They also added a gristmill to the operation.

The first newspaper published in Micanopy, the *Cotton States*, appeared in about 1860. It was founded by George J. Arnow and, initially, subscriptions to the Saturday morning weekly cost two dollars a year. Later, local newspapers included the *Micanopy Gazette* in the early 1880s; the *Tuscawilla News*, published by Thompson and Ruhl on Wednesdays, in the early 1890s; and in the mid-1920s, P.A. Ruhl's *Micanopy Herald*, which was printed in Gainesville but focused on news of Micanopy.

Micanopy played a part in the secession of Florida from the United States in 1861. From all of Alachua County, two men were appointed to attend the Secession Convention to determine the stand that Florida would take. One came from Gainesville, and the other was Dr. John C. Pelot of Micanopy. Pelot was elected as the convention's temporary chairman and he presented its opening address. The vote of those attending resulted in Florida's leaving the Union, and not long afterward it became one of the Confederate States of America.

In March 1867, Paynes Prairie flooded again, killing grazing sheep and cattle and once again turning the small, water-filled sinkholes into the huge Alachua Lake. The legislature declared it to be a navigable lake, preventing local residents from draining it and returning it to pastureland. However, the legislature could not prevent such an action on the part of Mother Nature. The water level began dropping in 1891, and in a final rush of water into the Alachua Sink in 1892, Alachua Lake was no more.

On December 26, 1894, not long after a period of temperatures in the eighties, a major freeze struck most of the state. Micanopy's temperature dropped to twenty-six degrees and the freeze lasted for thirty-six hours. Although some damage to the citrus crop was reported, a warm and wet January resulted in new shoots appearing on the trees. In February, a second freeze hit that practically wiped out the area's citrus industry. Sap froze in the trunks of orange trees and killed them. In 1899, when the few trees that remained were about to come back into production, even colder temperatures struck and essentially eliminated citrus from the region.

Micanopy had two telephone systems for a time. Its first was the East Florida Telephone Company, which was founded in 1904. Just two years later, Southern Bell also had an exchange in Micanopy, so one needed two separate telephones to be able to call everyone in town.

Micanopy was used as the setting of a mythical town in a major motion picture that opened in 1991. As the title character of *Doc Hollywood*, Michael J. Fox became stuck in the town on the way to a prestigious medical career in a big city. The new doctor eventually fell in love with the small-town atmosphere and its annual squash festival and decided to stay. Other stars of the movie included Mary Steenburgen and Rip Torn. Several local sites and residents were seen on-screen, introducing the public to the quaint little town, which is not very different from what was shown in the movie.

Today, Micanopy attracts history buffs, antiques enthusiasts and the curious who wish to spend a little time in a peaceful place that the hectic pace of modern life appears to have overlooked. A brief visit to the historical museum located in the old warehouse will give you a glimpse of what Micanopy used to look like, and when you come back out, you may be surprised to see how little things have changed in a century or more.

People

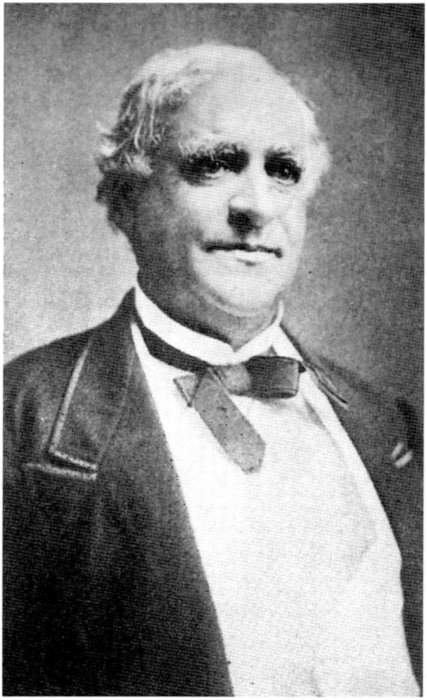

DAVID LEVY YULEE
Levy worked on his father's Providence Plantation near Micanopy before becoming Florida's first senator. He built the first railroad to cross the state. *Image courtesy of the Florida Photographic Collection.*

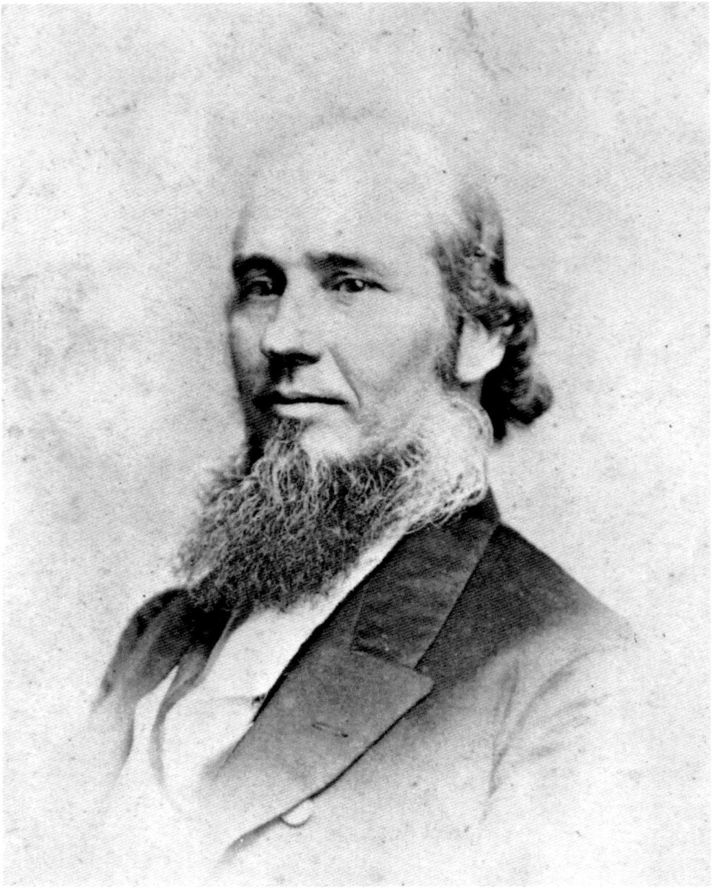

GEORGE MEANS

Judge George W. Means grew citrus and served as a trustee of the Micanopy Presbyterian Church. He and his wife donated land for its construction. *Image courtesy of the Florida Photographic Collection.*

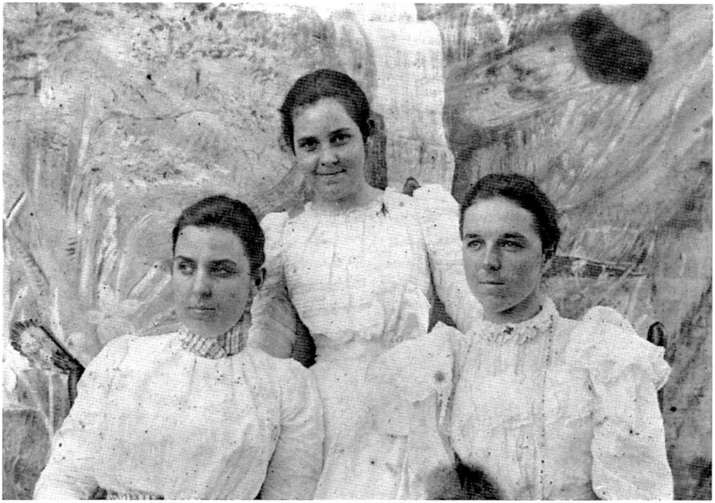

CORA AND ZOLA JOLLY AND EDNA PARDEE

On the right is Edna Pardee, one of the sisters who ran a private school in the 1880s just west of the Tuscawilla Hotel. Also shown are Cora and Zola Jolly. *Image courtesy of the Florida Photographic Collection.*

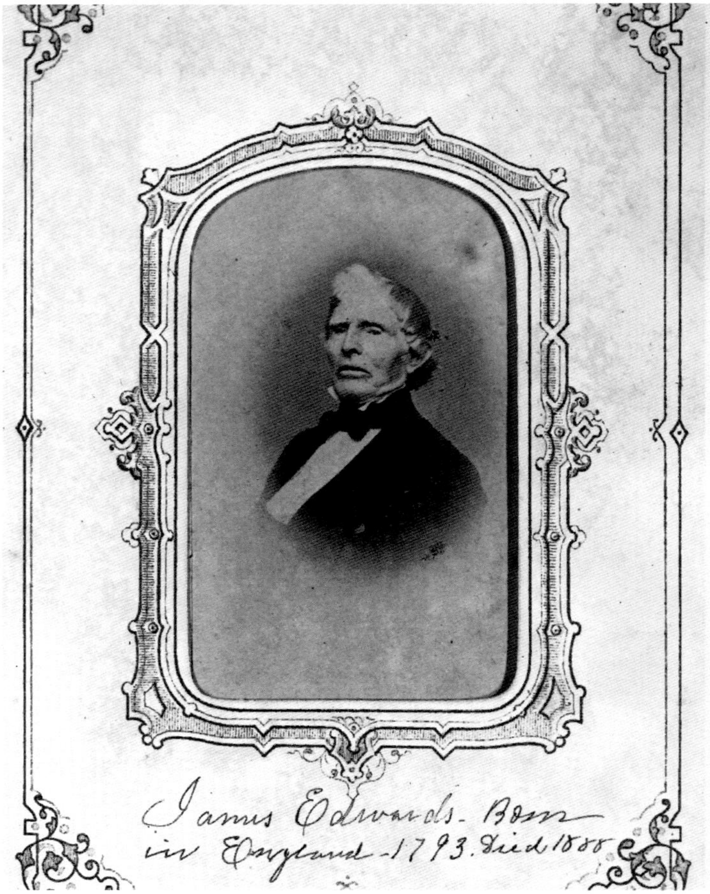

JAMES EDWARDS

Edwards was one of the first to settle in the Arredondo Grant. Born in Devonshire, England, he came to the United States in 1819 and to this area in 1822. *Image courtesy of the Florida Photographic Collection.*

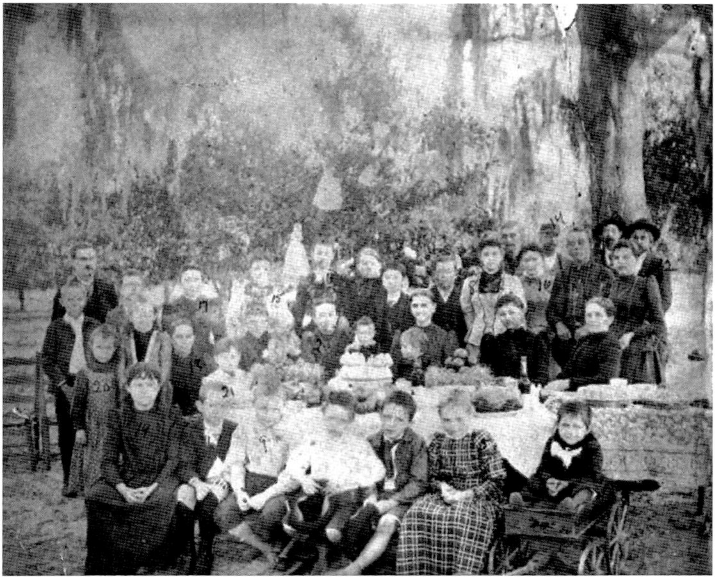

CHRISTMAS CELEBRATION
This 1892 holiday gathering hosted by the Croxtons at Croxton Park, on the way to Rochelle included Pardees, Zetrouers, Turners, Merrys and others. *Image courtesy of the Florida Photographic Collection.*

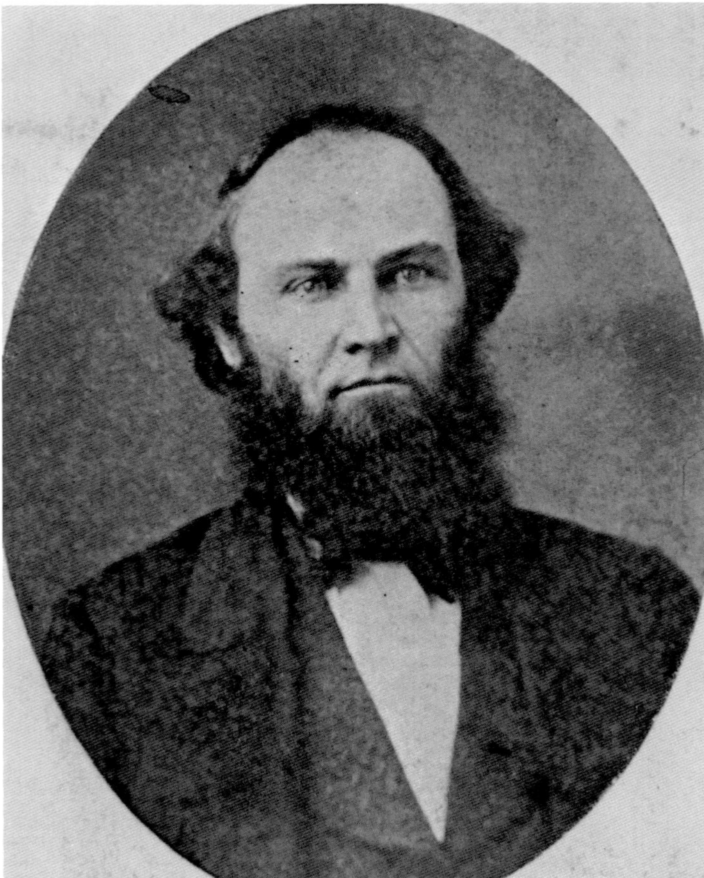

WILLIAM EDWARDS

William's father, James Edwards, fled the area in 1835 during the Second Seminole War. He returned to Micanopy to live with William in 1865. *Image courtesy of the Florida Photographic Collection.*

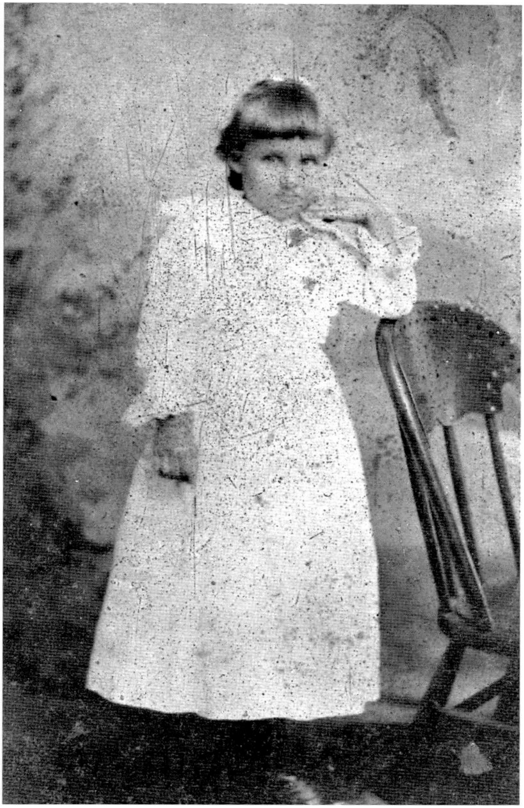

HAYDEE CROXTON

Haydee was the daughter of James Mintor Croxton and Mary Beulah Pardee Croxton. She married Andrew Joel Walker. *Image courtesy of the Florida Photographic Collection.*

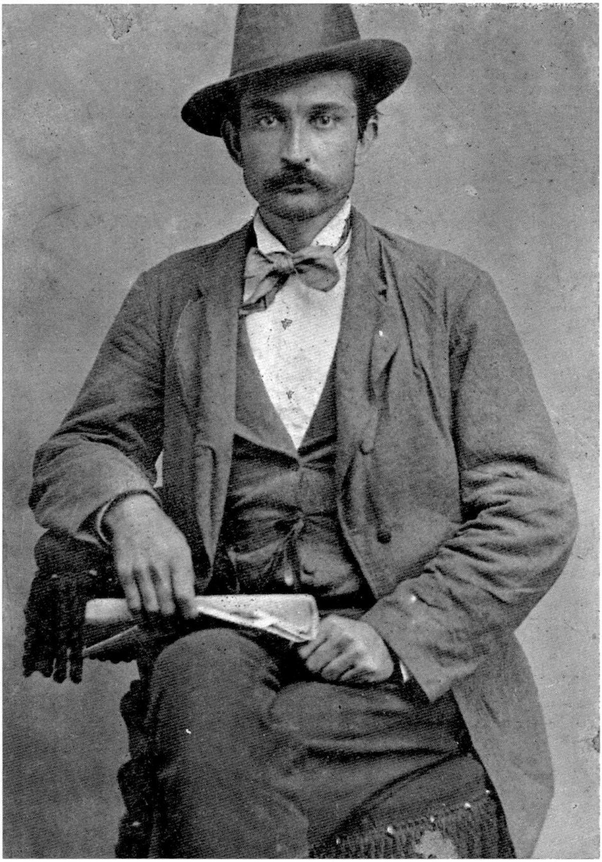

JAMES MINTOR CROXTON

James piloted the steamboat *Chacala* on Alachua Lake during the early 1890s. He was an officer in the Masons and served as the county surveyor in 1909. *Image courtesy of the Florida Photographic Collection.*

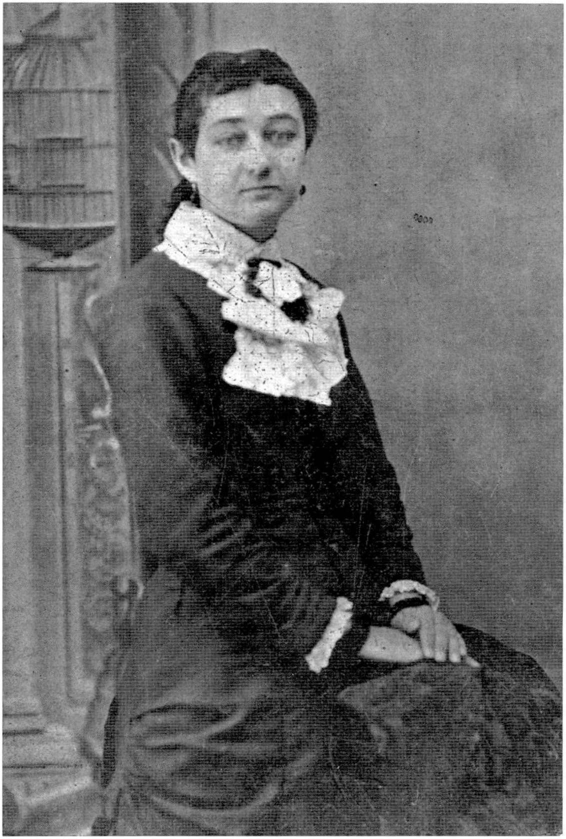

MARY BEULAH PARDEE CROXTON
Mary was the second wife of James Mintor Croxton and the mother of Haydee Croxton, Harry James Croxton and Marion Hatti Croxton. *Image courtesy of the Florida Photographic Collection.*

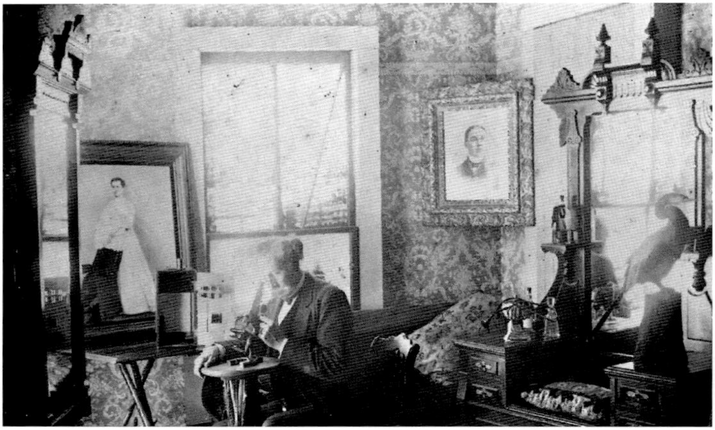

Montgomery Laboratory

Dr. Lucius Montgomery is shown here in his laboratory, which was located in his home. He came to the area in 1868 and also raised oranges. *Image courtesy of the Florida Photographic Collection.*

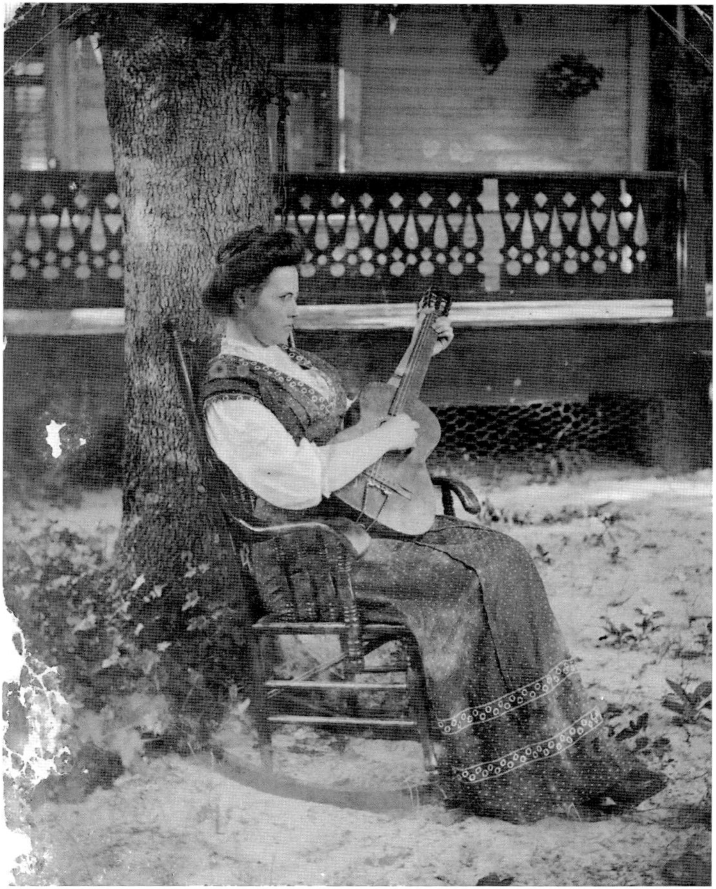

MARTHA CHAMBERLIN

George Chamberlin fought in the Civil War and settled in Micanopy. This is his daughter, Martha, who typed and played piano and guitar despite being blind. *Image courtesy of the Florida Photographic Collection.*

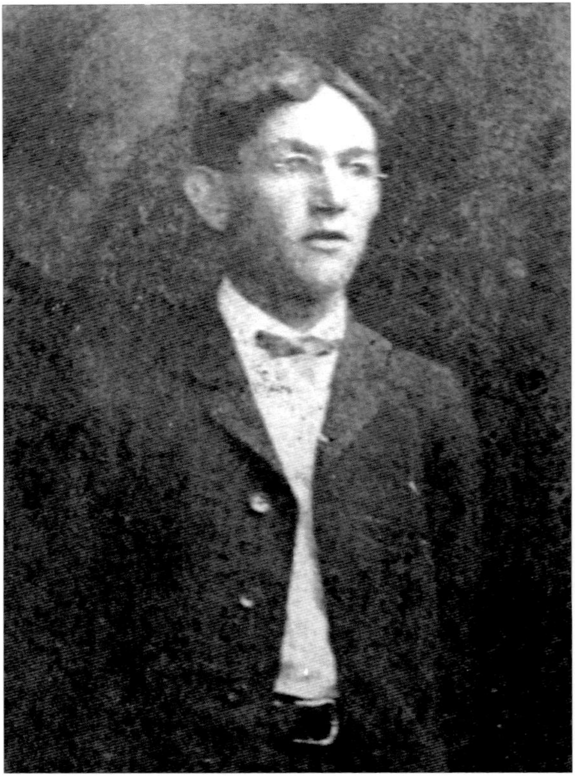

ROBERT ARNOW

This is Micanopy native and county deputy sheriff Robert E. Arnow. He was fatally shot in 1921 at age thirty-three, while attempting to arrest John Bowyer. *Image courtesy of the Florida Photographic Collection.*

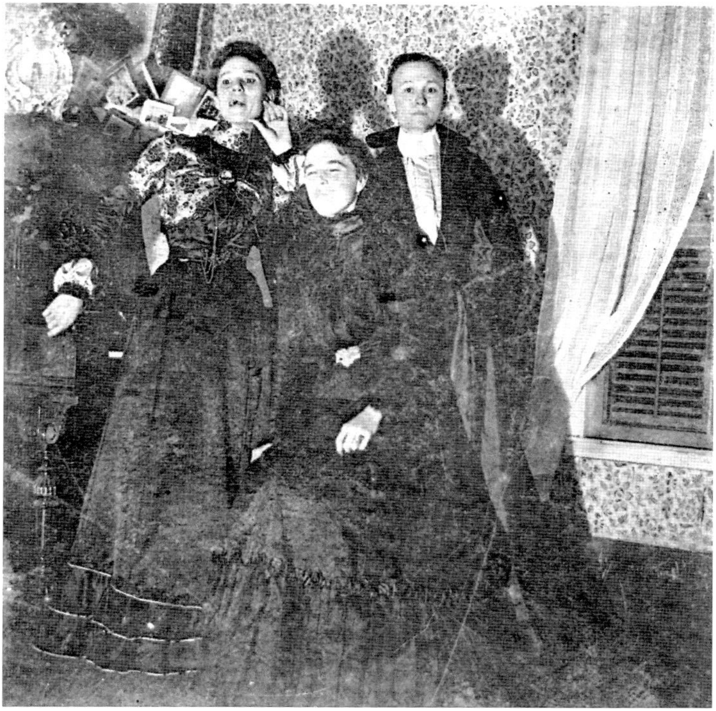

PARDEE FAMILY
Dr. Pardee was one of the early prominent citrus growers in Micanopy, with groves producing in the 1880s. Shown here are daughters Edna and Emma and a friend. *Image courtesy of the Florida Photographic Collection.*

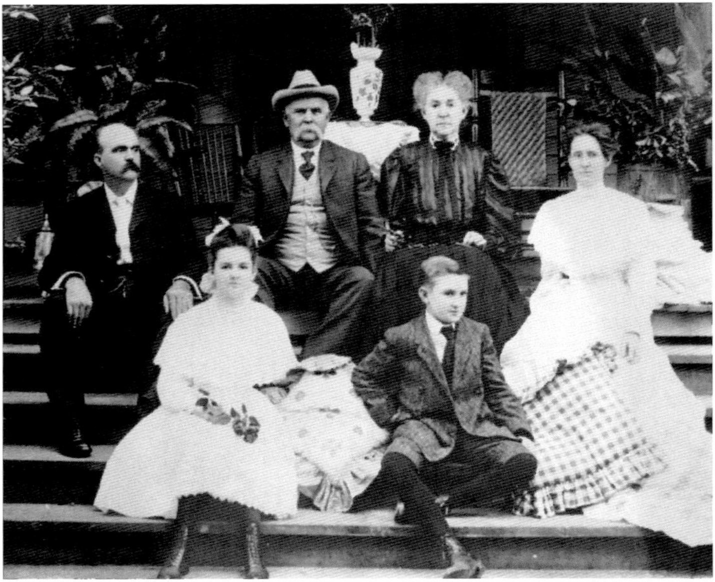

BARR FAMILY

John Jacob Barr built his home in about 1870 with lovely gardens. He is shown here on the top step with his wife, Sue, and other family members. *Image courtesy of the Florida Photographic Collection.*

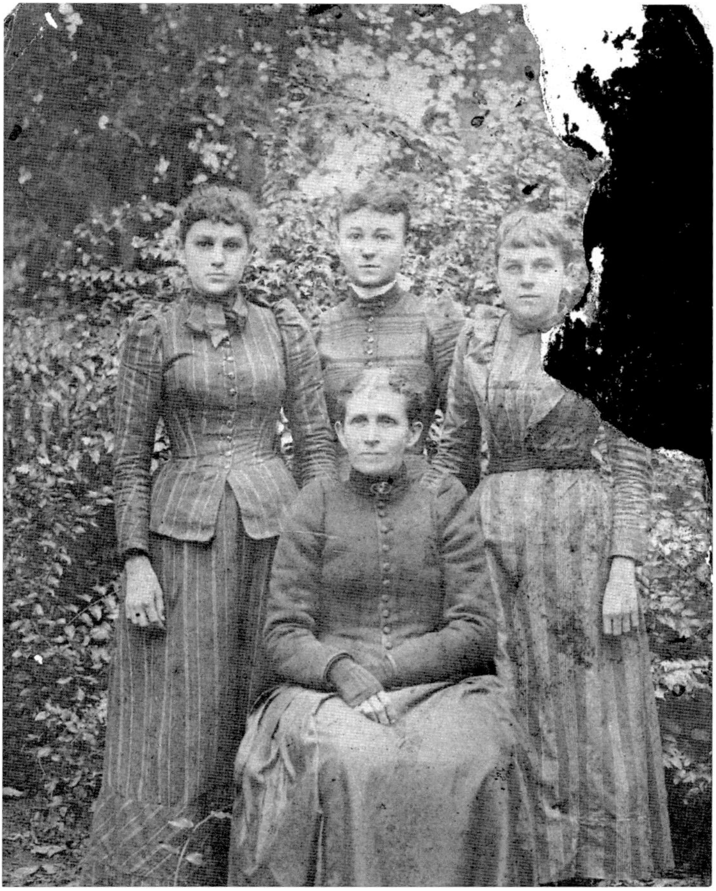

PARDEE WOMEN
Standing left to right are sisters Emma Pardee, Edna Addison Pardee and Honoria Pardee. Seated is their mother, Carolina Bethany Turner Pardee. *Image courtesy of the Florida Photographic Collection.*

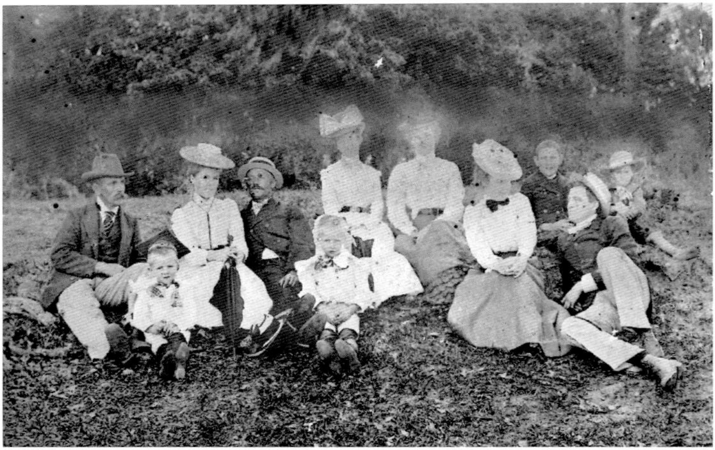

Picnic

This 1909 picnic by Lake Tuscawilla included the children of several prominent citizens of Micanopy, including Leon Thrasher and Arthur Chitty. *Image courtesy of the Florida Photographic Collection.*

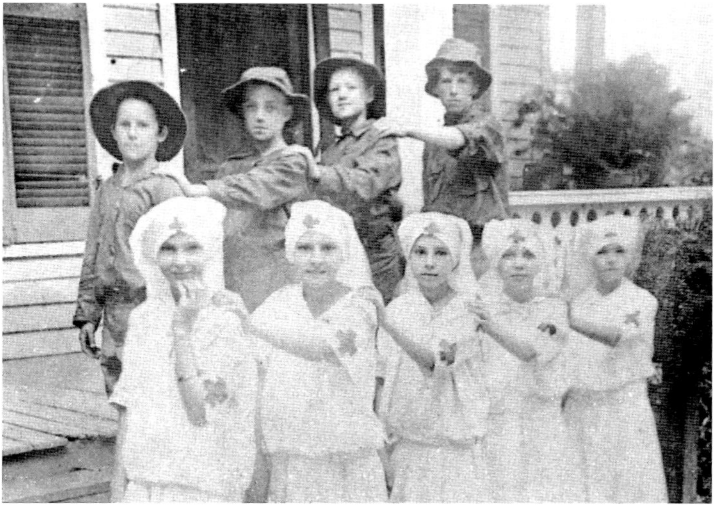

CHILDREN DRESSED AS SOLDIERS AND NURSES
While most of the world was preparing to enter World War I, these Micanopy youngsters dressed up to emulate our doughboys and nurses. *Image courtesy of the Florida Photographic Collection.*

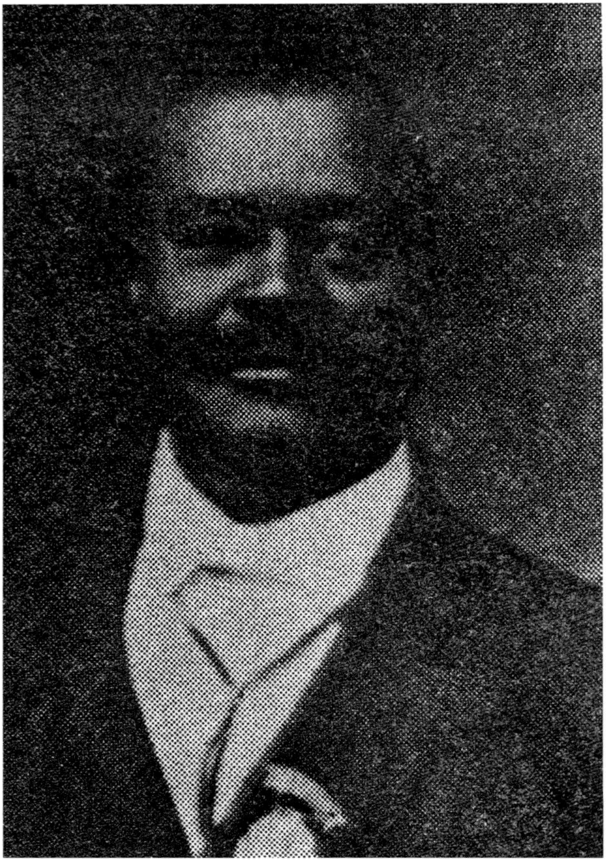

JOHN WALTER DUKES
Reverend Dukes was in Micanopy in 1883–87, leading a mission for the AME church. He later moved on to Ocala, Tampa, Apopka and Eatonville. *Image courtesy of the Florida Photographic Collection.*

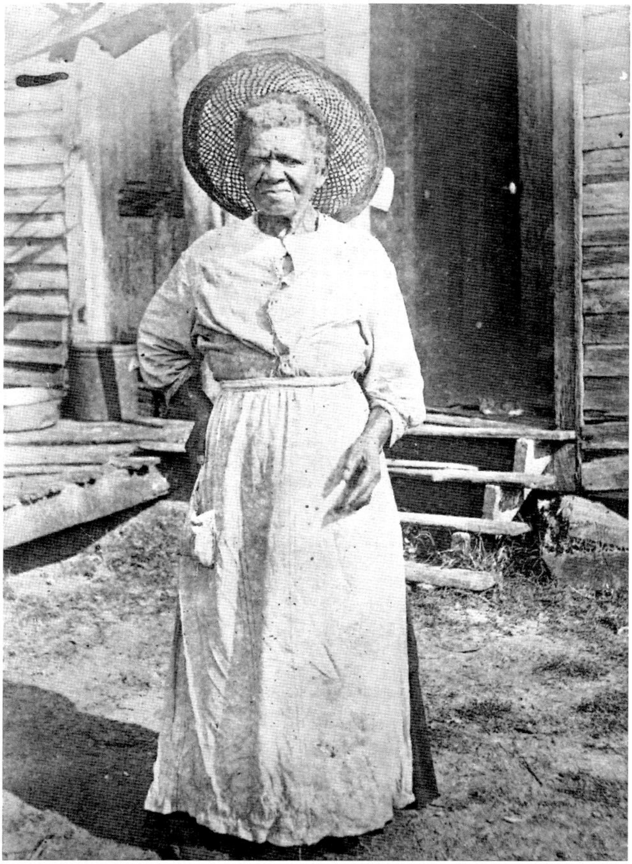

SELENA ROLLINS
Born in 1837, Selena was one of the former slaves who settled in Micanopy. When she died in 1925, she was the last surviving former slave there. *Image courtesy of the Florida Photographic Collection.*

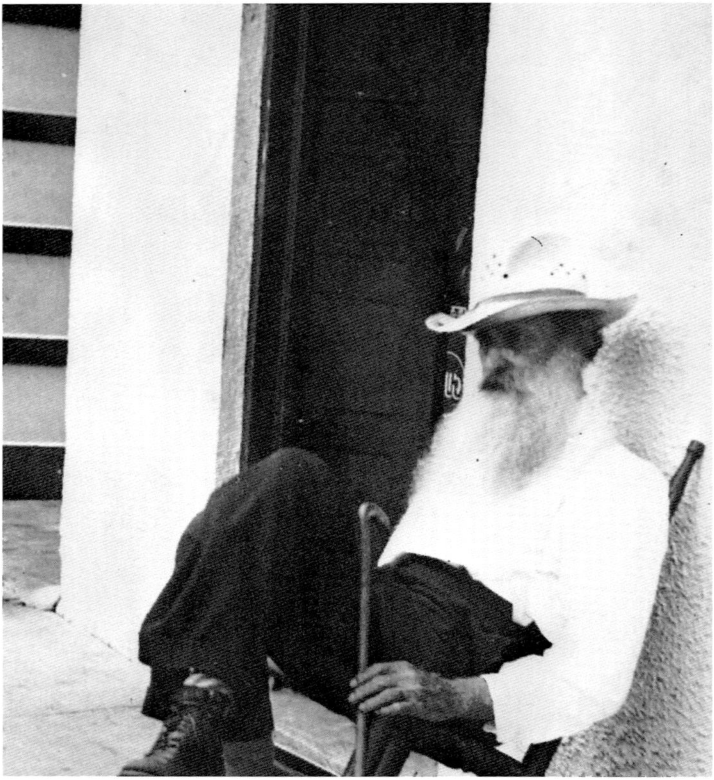

John K. Feaster

This Micanopy native was educated at Emory University and then returned to his hometown to farm. He is pictured here relaxing in 1939, six years before he was buried in the private Feaster cemetery. *Image courtesy of the Florida Photographic Collection.*

Around Micanopy

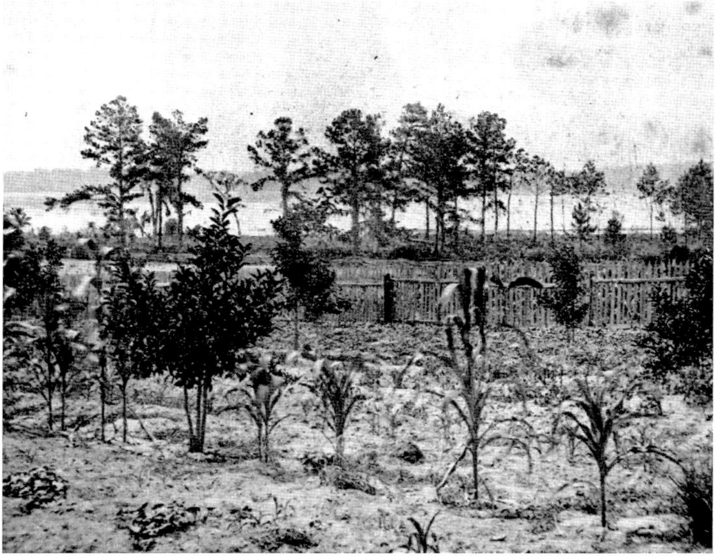

LAKE TUSCAWILLA
This large lake southeast of downtown Micanopy takes its name from Cuscowilla, a mid-1700s Oconee village on its shore led by Chief Cowkeeper. *Image courtesy of the Florida Photographic Collection.*

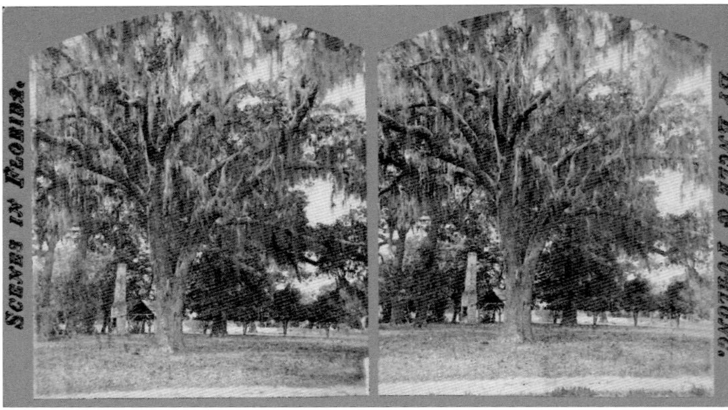

Seminole War Headquarters

Photographed in the 1870s, this site was the army headquarters during the 1830s. Nearby battles included Welika Pond, Fort Drane and Kanapaha Prairie. *Image courtesy of the Florida Photographic Collection.*

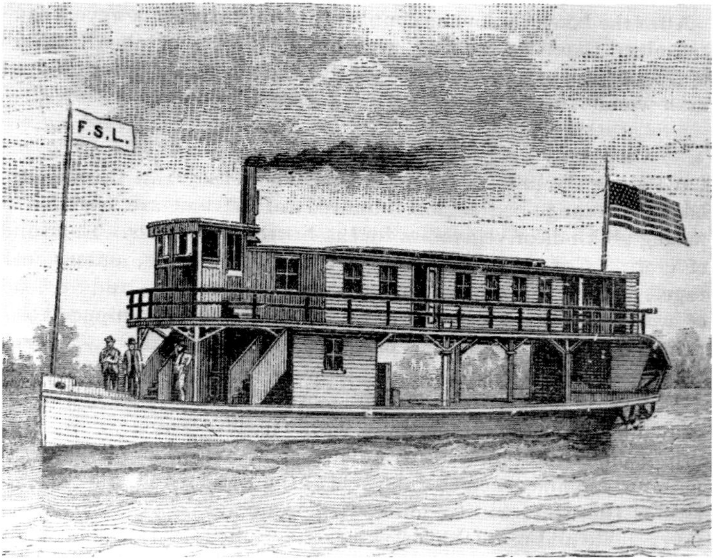

F.S. Lewis

Until 1892, this and other steamboats were used to cross the large Alachua Lake. After its drain became unplugged and the lake disappeared, it turned into a prairie. *Image courtesy of the Florida Photographic Collection.*

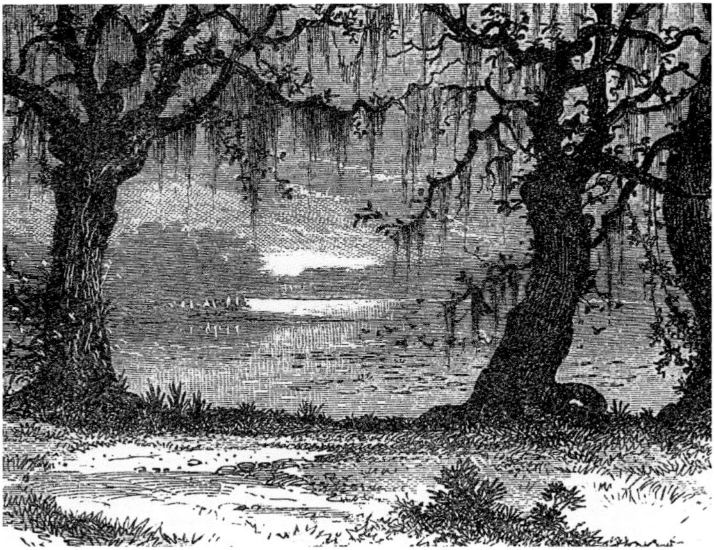

"Big Jug" Sinkhole

This 1883 engraving shows the sinkhole north of Micanopy that was plugged from 1871 to 1891 and flooded Paynes Prairie to create Alachua Lake. *Image courtesy of the Florida Photographic Collection.*

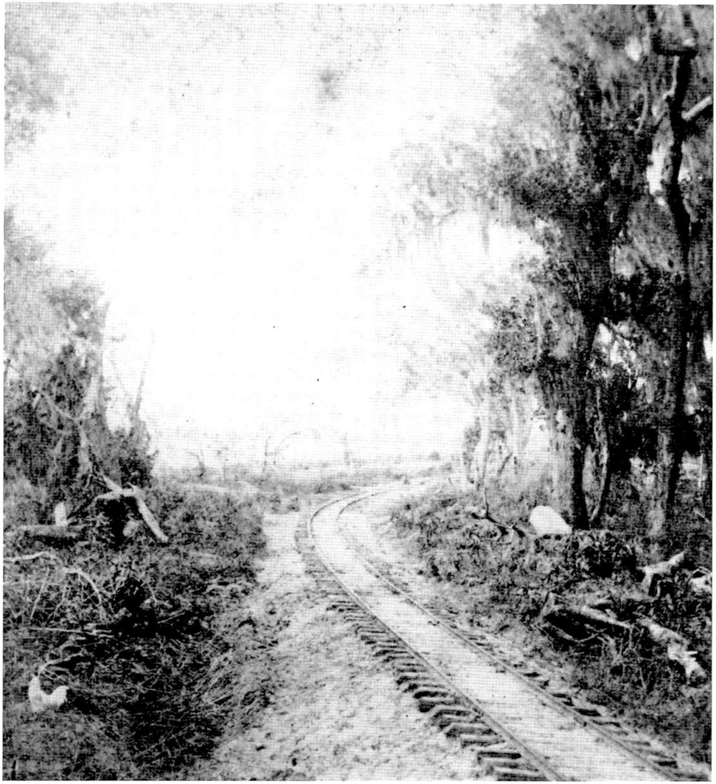

FLORIDA SOUTHERN RAILROAD
Starting in 1881, the main line of the railroad connected Gainesville with Micanopy's neighbor town, Rochelle. These tracks ran through Paynes Prairie. *Image courtesy of the Florida Photographic Collection.*

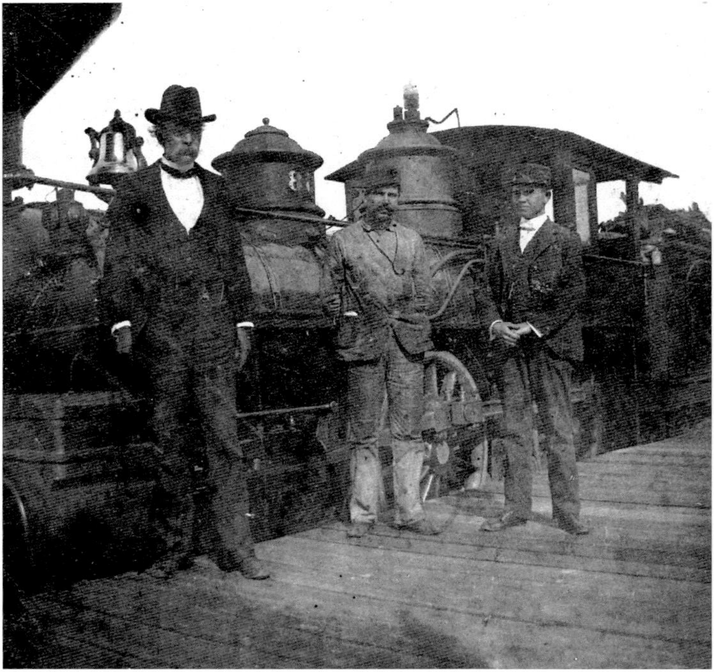

MICANOPY JUNCTION

Dr. Lucius Montgomery is shown here with an engineer and fireman at Micanopy Junction, where one could board a train going all the way to New York. *Image courtesy of the Florida Photographic Collection.*

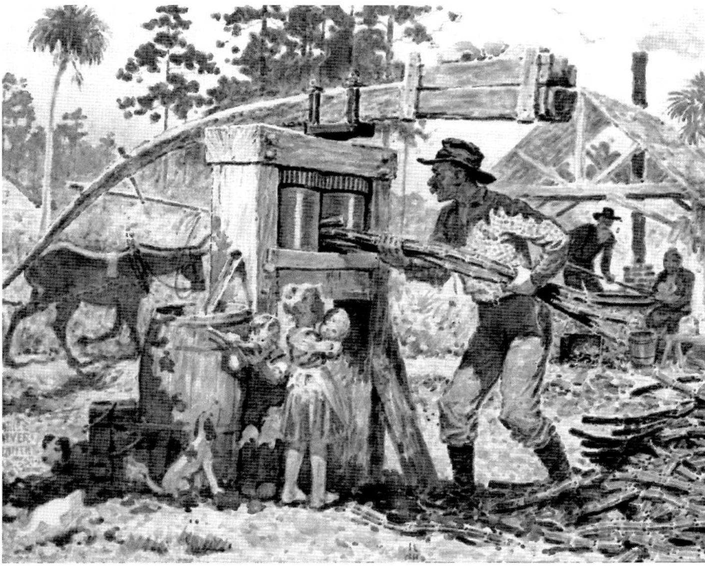

SUGAR CANE GRINDING
This is a watercolor painted by James Calvert Smith, who grew up in nearby Tacoma. It depicts the 1880s production of sugar in Alachua County. *Image courtesy of the Florida Photographic Collection.*

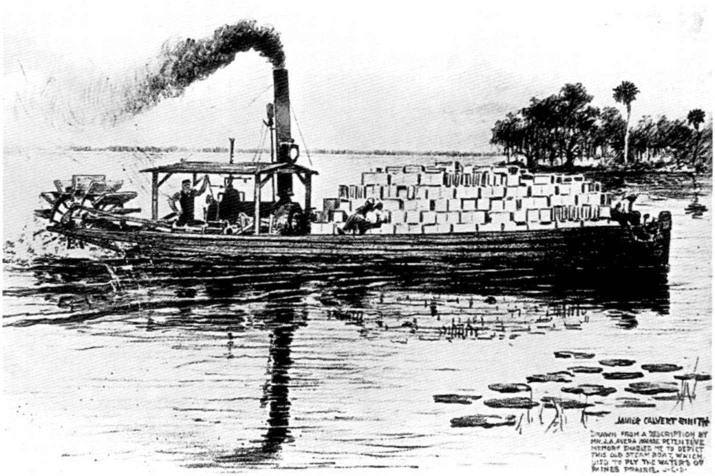

Paddle Wheel Steamboat

James Calvert Smith drew this sketch of a stern-wheeler, the main way to transport crops across Alachua Lake to the main railroad before the spur track was laid. *Image courtesy of the Florida Photographic Collection.*

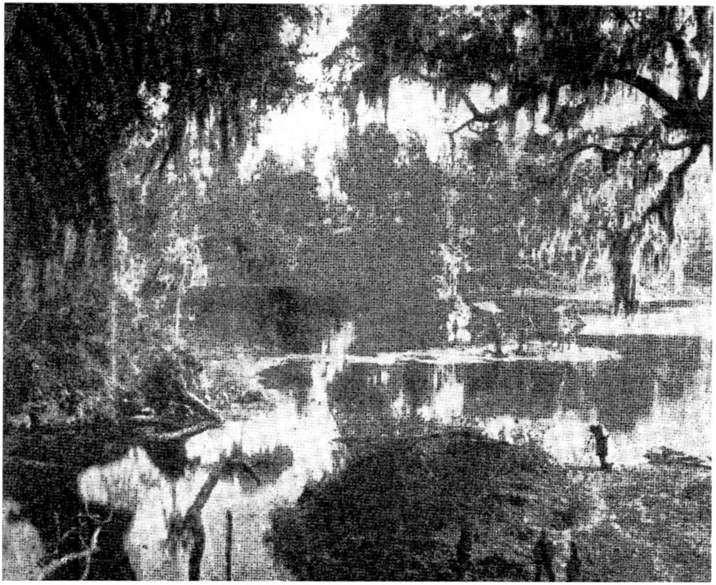

ALACHUA LAKE

At times, Paynes Prairie has been flooded as Alachua Lake. The name comes from the La Chua cattle ranch, named for an American Indian word meaning "jug." *Image courtesy of the Florida Photographic Collection.*

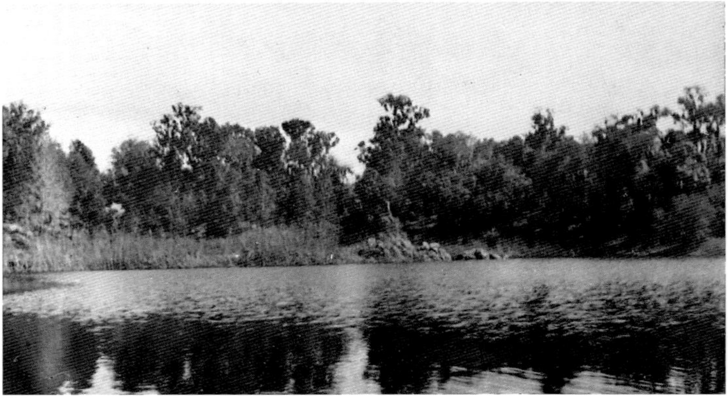

ALACHUA SINK

The sinkhole between Micanopy and Gainesville was known to the Spanish as La Chua, meaning "jug." They applied that name to their cattle ranch nearby. *Image courtesy of the Florida Photographic Collection.*

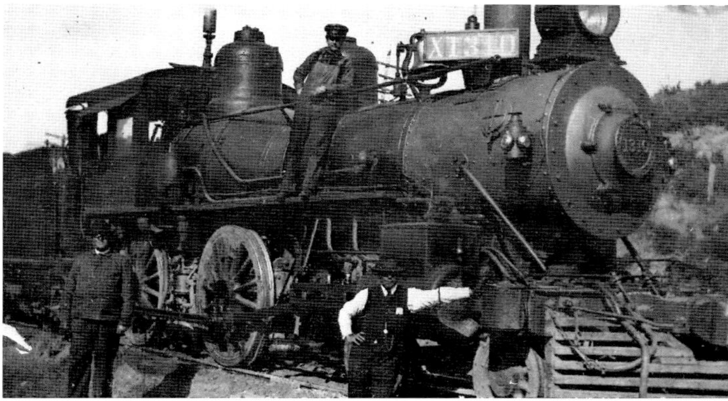

RAILROAD ENGINE

Photographed at Micanopy Junction, where the spur line to Micanopy met the main tracks, is Southern Pacific's Engine 1310, built in 1880. *Image courtesy of the Florida Photographic Collection.*

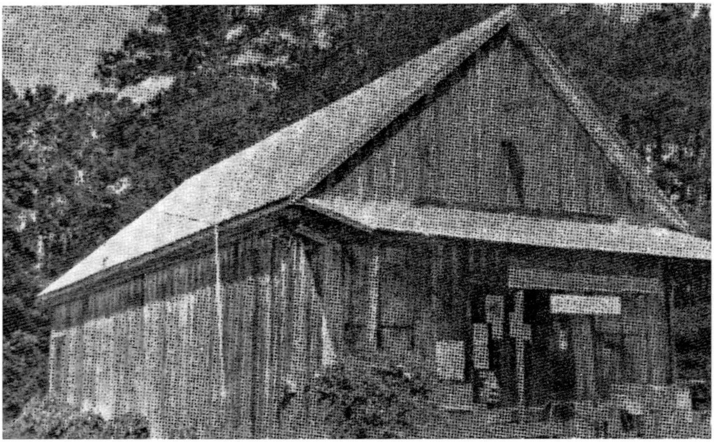

Evinston

Within walking distance of Micanopy is the town of Evinston. Shown here is its post office, essentially unchanged after more than a century. *Image courtesy of the Florida Photographic Collection.*

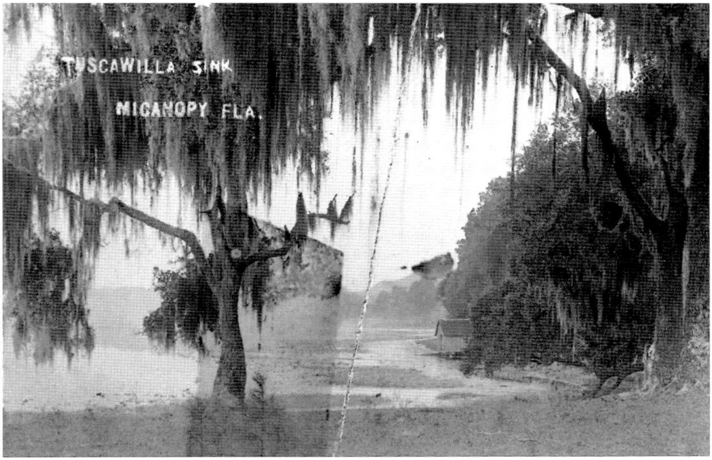

TUSCAWILLA SINK

When William Bartram visited this area in 1774, he called it the Alachua Savanna. He found no trees, and cattle grazed among horses and deer. *Image courtesy of the Florida Photographic Collection.*

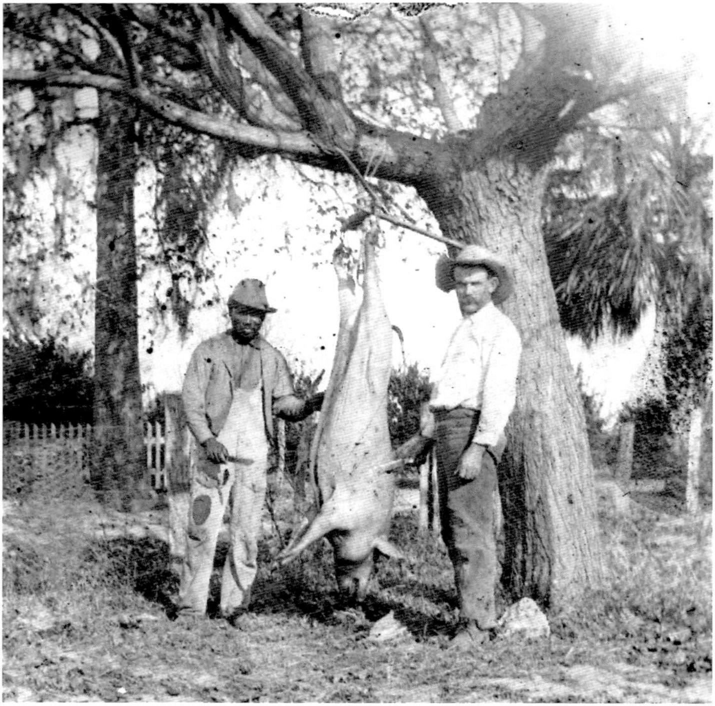

HOG BUTCHERING

Henry White and Jack Hare are shown here in 1913 butchering a hog. The site is believed to be the Leitner estate along Lake Levy, northwest of downtown. *Image courtesy of the Florida Photographic Collection.*

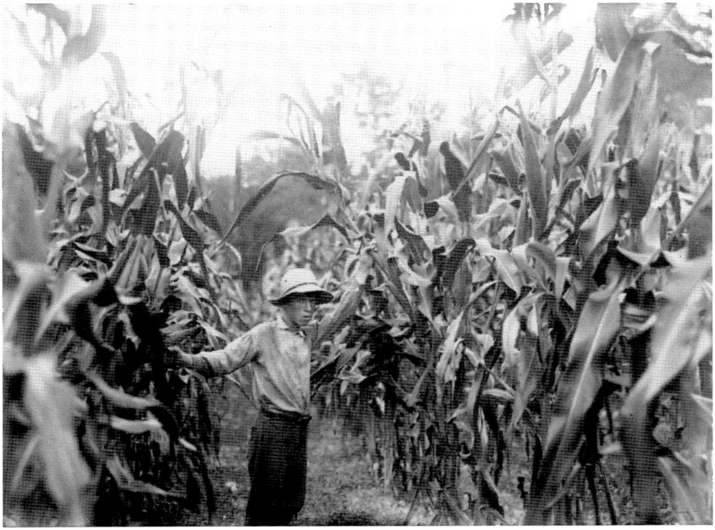

CORNFIELD
Tom Feaster is shown here in 1917 in a field of tall corn. It was being grown as a project of the University of Florida Agricultural Experiment Station. *Image courtesy of the Florida Photographic Collection.*

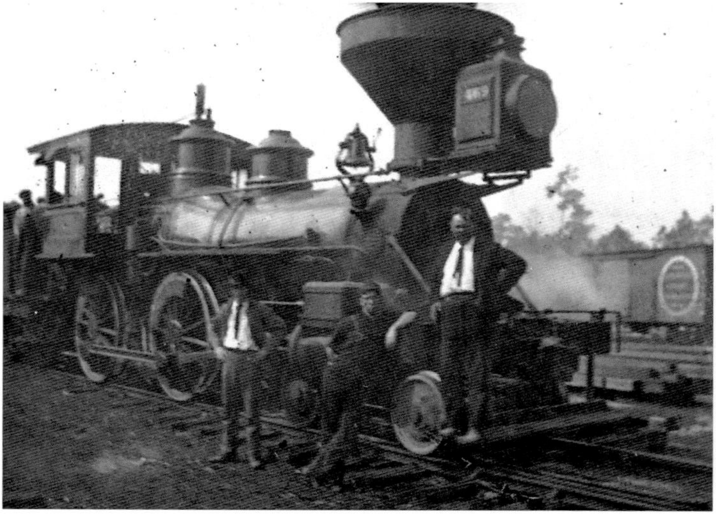

Railroad Engine

This train engine at Micanopy Junction was No. 469 of the Savannah, Florida and Western Railroad. It was built in Baldwin in 1883. *Image courtesy of the Florida Photographic Collection.*

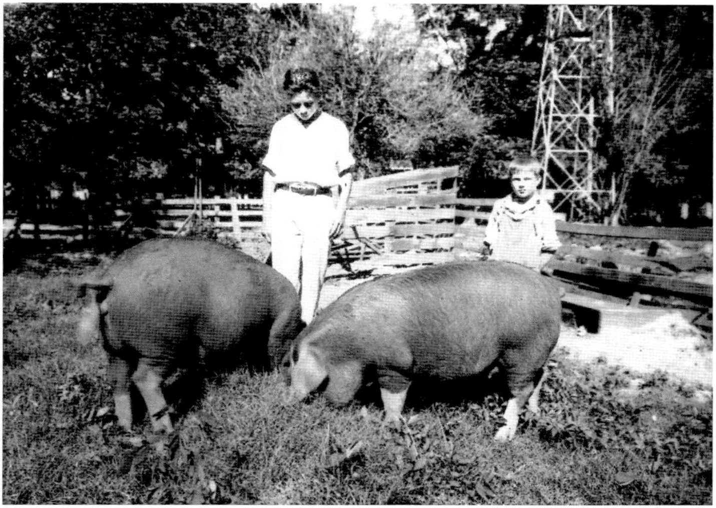

HERLONG PIGS

In 1910, Natalie Simonton married wealthy entrepreneur Zetty C. Herlong. They bought and enlarged a small house and raised Poland China pigs. *Image courtesy of the Florida Photographic Collection.*

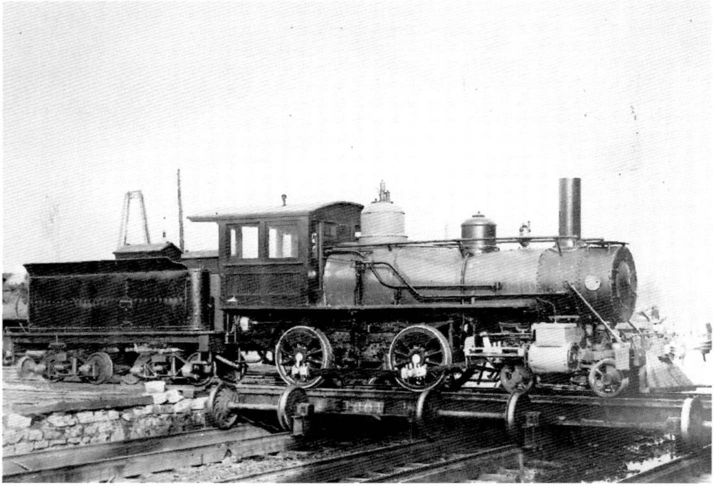

MELTON LUMBER COMPANY TRAIN

This local company with a three-mile track owned this engine beginning in 1912. It was owned by the Escambia Mill Company when photographed in 1920. *Image courtesy of the Florida Photographic Collection.*

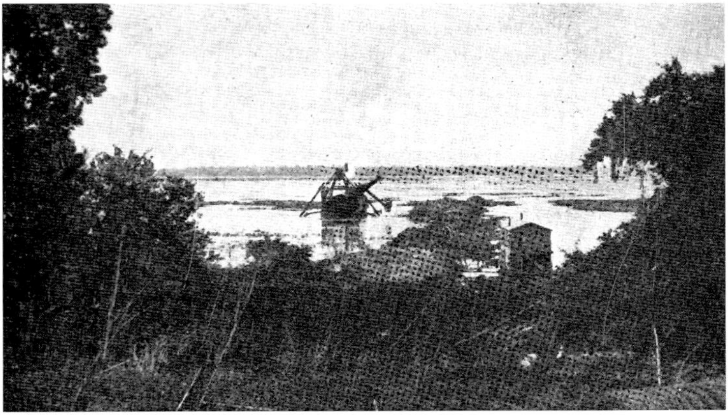

DREDGE

In the mid-1920s, U.S. Highway 441, which passes by Micanopy, was extended across Paynes Prairie. This is one of the dredges used in the project. *Image courtesy of the Florida Photographic Collection.*

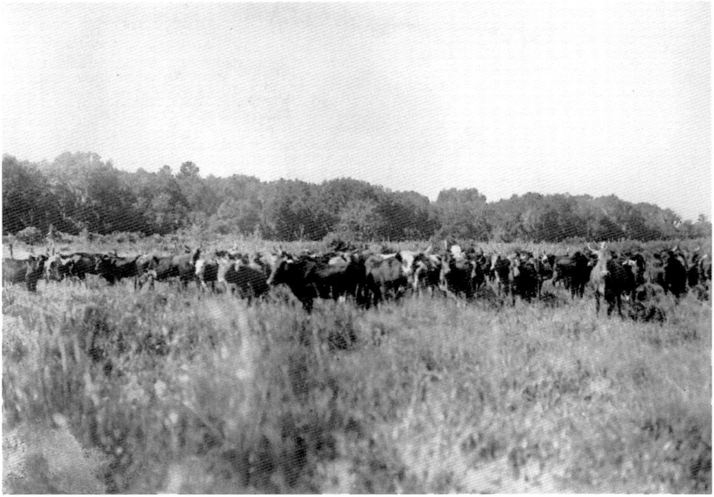

Cattle on Paynes Prairie

Paynes Prairie has been a successful cattle pasture. Shown here grazing in 1932 are cows of the University of Florida Agricultural Experiment Station. *Image courtesy of the Florida Photographic Collection.*

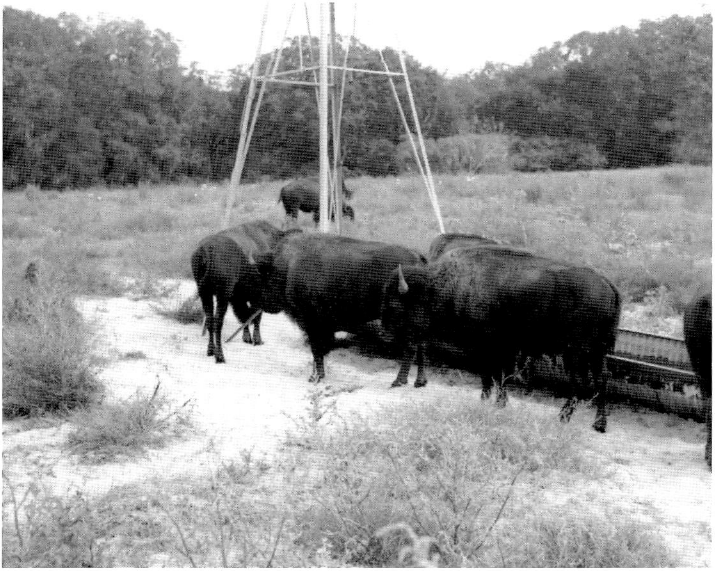

BISON AT PAYNES PRAIRIE

Bison are shown here in 1976, a year after ten of them were brought from Oklahoma. They slowly increased in numbers on Paynes Prairie. *Image courtesy of the Florida Photographic Collection.*

Businesses

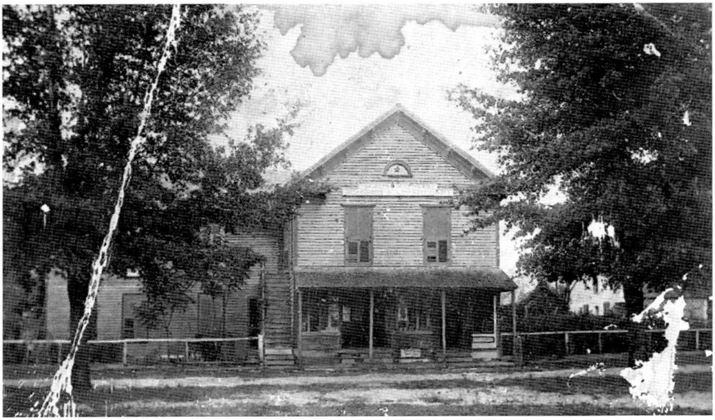

COOPER AND MATHERS DRUGS AND APOTHECARY
James Cooper and Augustus Mathers opened this store in 1853. It was rebuilt after a fire, served as the Palm Inn and burned again in about 1935. *Image courtesy of the Florida Photographic Collection.*

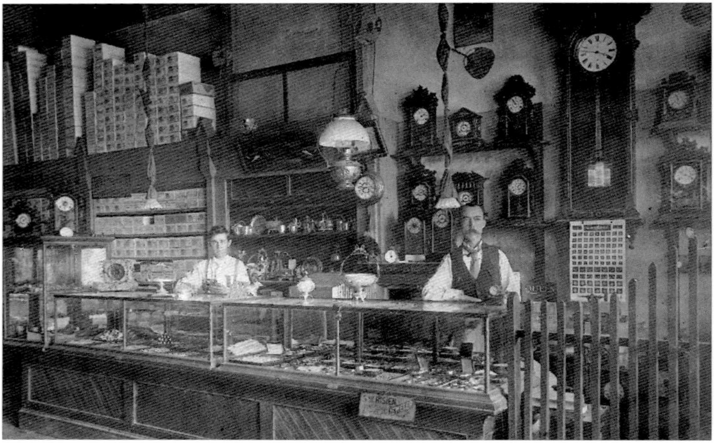

Benjamin Store

Simon H. Benjamin and John E. Thrasher formed a partnership to own and operate this store. Shown here in 1893 is their inventory of jewelry and clocks. *Image courtesy of the Florida Photographic Collection.*

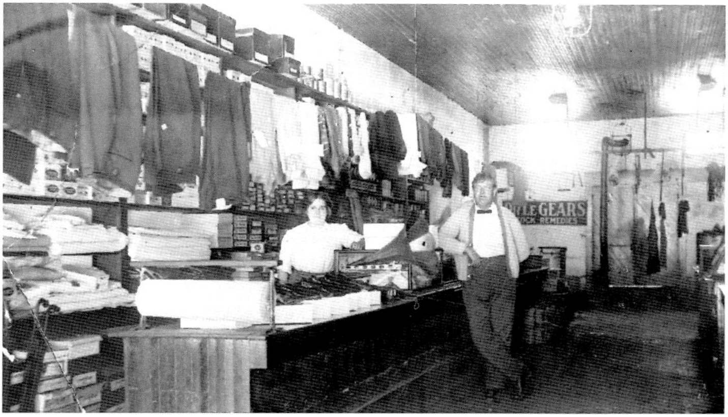

CHITTY STORE

Edward Cooper Chitty owned a general merchandise store in the Benjamin Building. Here at work in it are Dora Mae Chitty and Sam I. Chitty. *Image courtesy of the Florida Photographic Collection.*

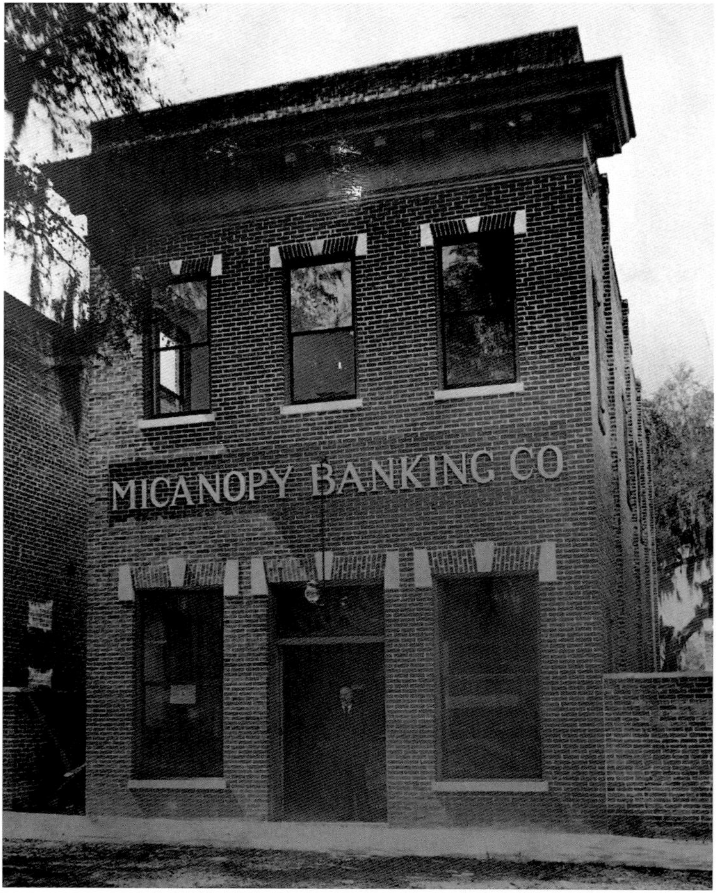

Micanopy Banking Company

John Jacob Barr founded the bank and built this structure in 1906 to house it. The marble and iron grills of tellers' cages and a large vault remain. *Image courtesy of the Florida Photographic Collection.*

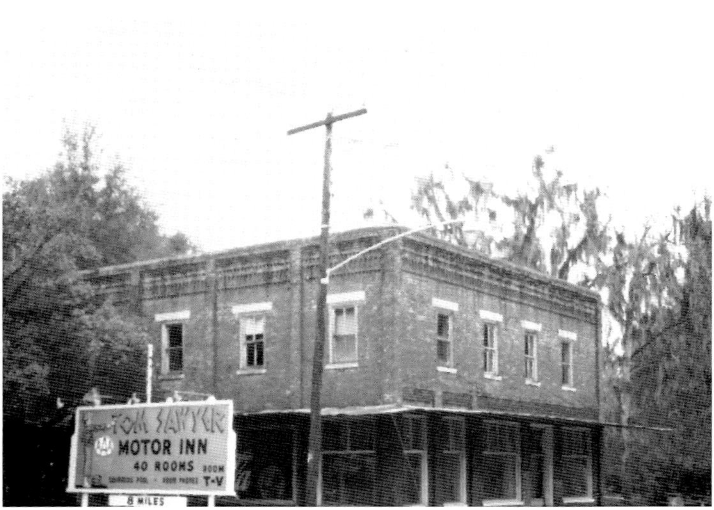

FONTAINE STORE

This clothing, dry goods and grocery store was built in about 1900 by Benjamin Fontaine. It closed in the early 1930s and was razed in 1962. *Image courtesy of the Florida Photographic Collection.*

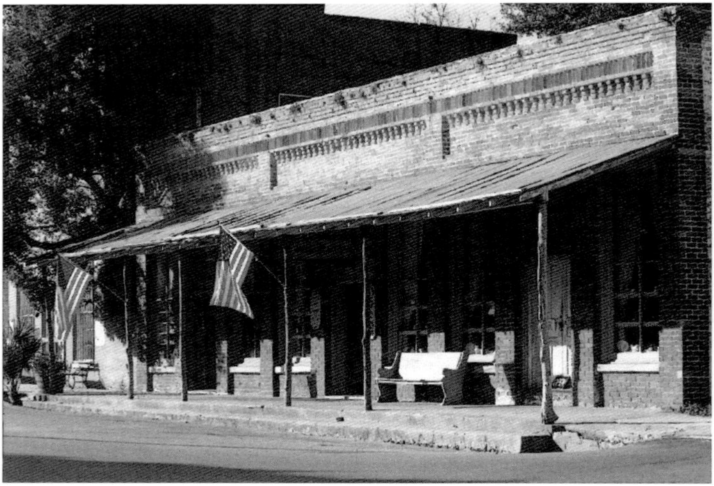

Benjamin Building

Although this was the town's first brick building, it was still partially destroyed by fire. It was rebuilt with the single story as shown here. *Image courtesy of the Florida Photographic Collection.*

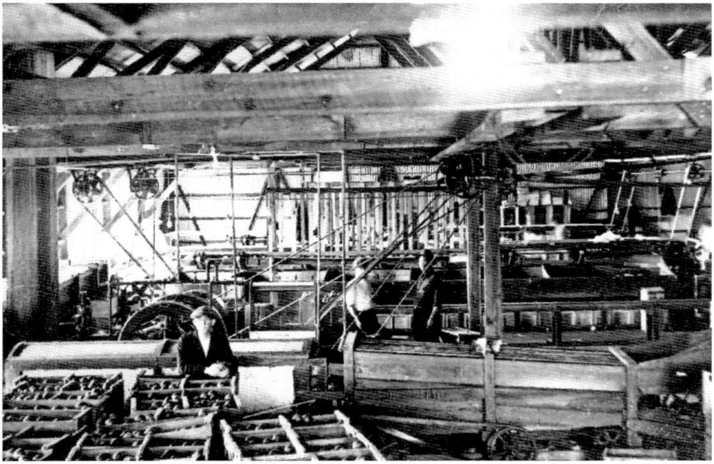

MICANOPY PACKING COMPANY

Here, oranges for shipment were wrapped in dark beige paper with a red circular "Micanopy" stamp. The sorter and electric lights were run by a gas engine. *Image courtesy of the Florida Photographic Collection.*

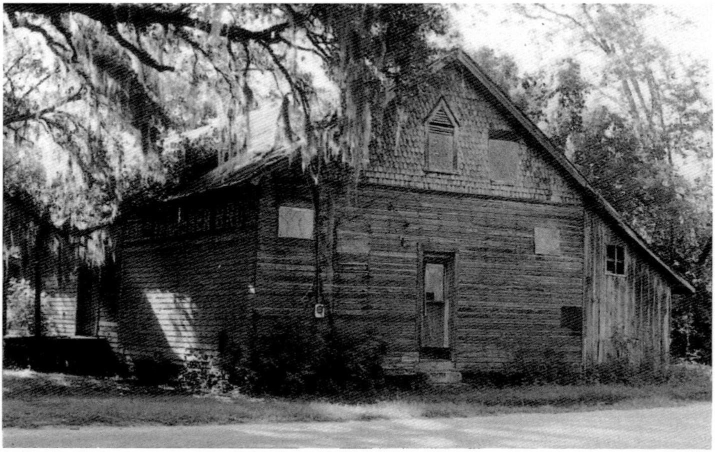

Thrasher Warehouse

J.E. Thrasher built this in about 1890 along the railroad tracks that ran by its service platform. It is now the home of the Micanopy Historical Society Museum. *Image courtesy of the Florida Photographic Collection.*

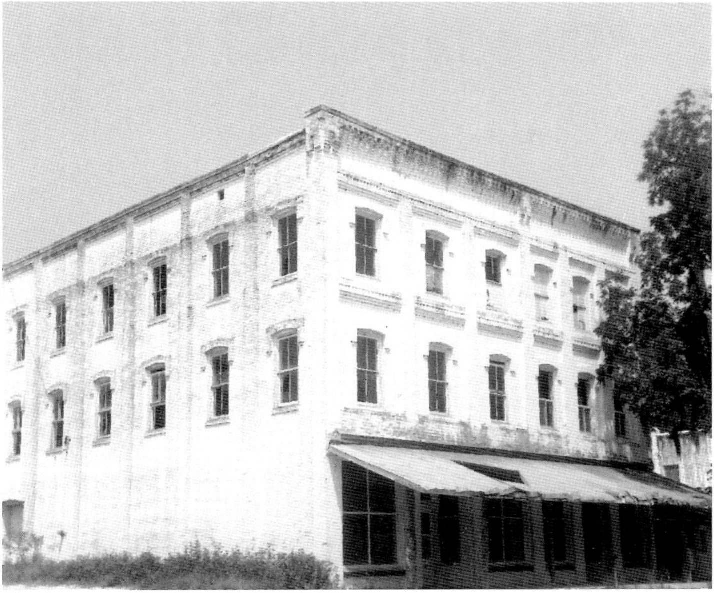

FEASTER BUILDING

Otis Feaster built this in 1903, and the first floor held a general store, drugstore and telephone office. The third floor served as Micanopy's opera house. *Image courtesy of the Florida Photographic Collection.*

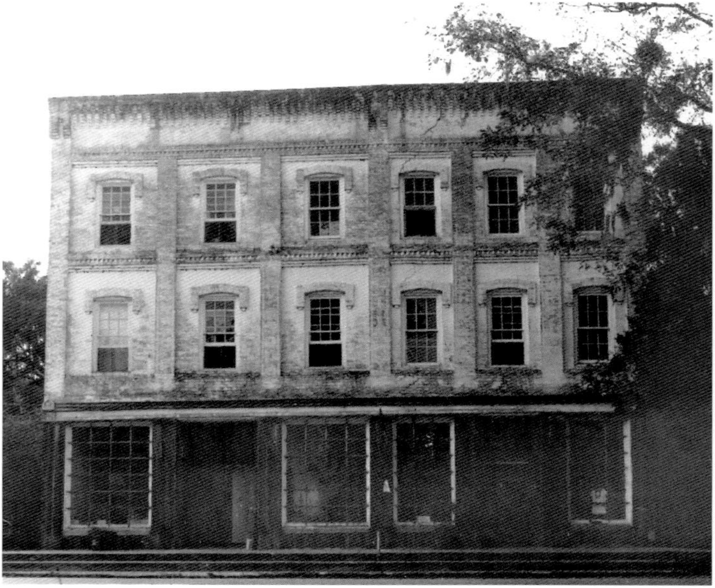

Feaster Building

In the early days, the Micanopy post office was located in this building. It later housed an art gallery and is presently an antique store. *Image courtesy of the Florida Photographic Collection.*

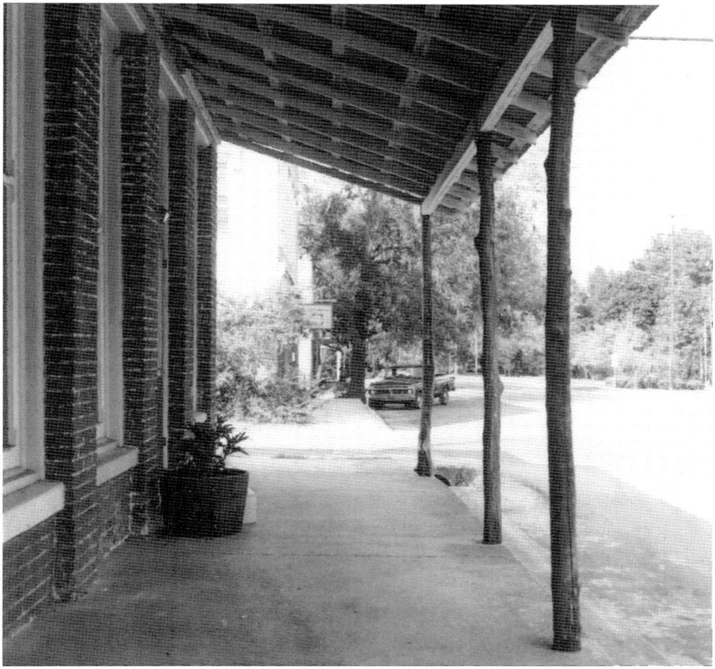

BENJAMIN BUILDING

A shed porch makes this one of very few Micanopy buildings with a shaded sidewalk. Inside are O. Brisky Books and Dakota Mercantile. *Image courtesy of the Florida Photographic Collection.*

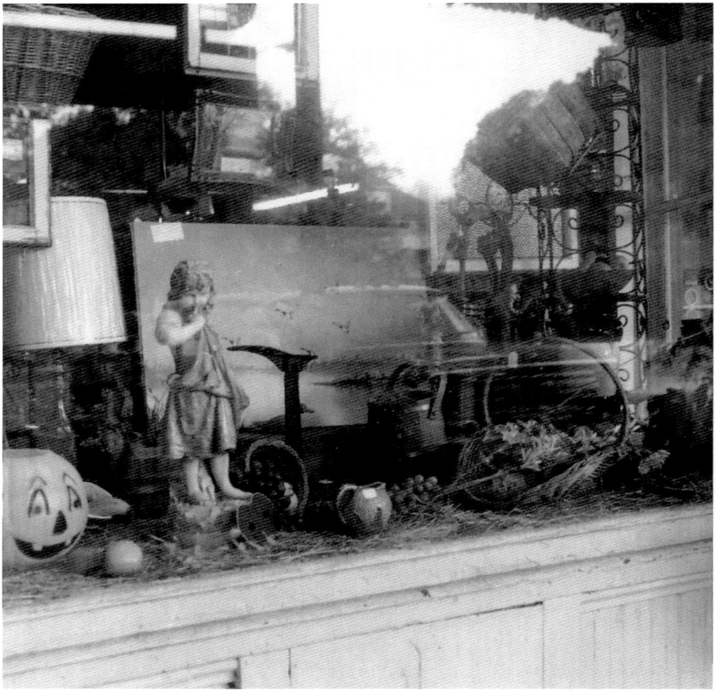

MOTT-MAY BUILDING

Erected prior to 1900, this was a general store for over seventy years. A window display is shown from the 1970s, when Sylvia Lewis sold antiques here. *Image courtesy of the Florida Photographic Collection.*

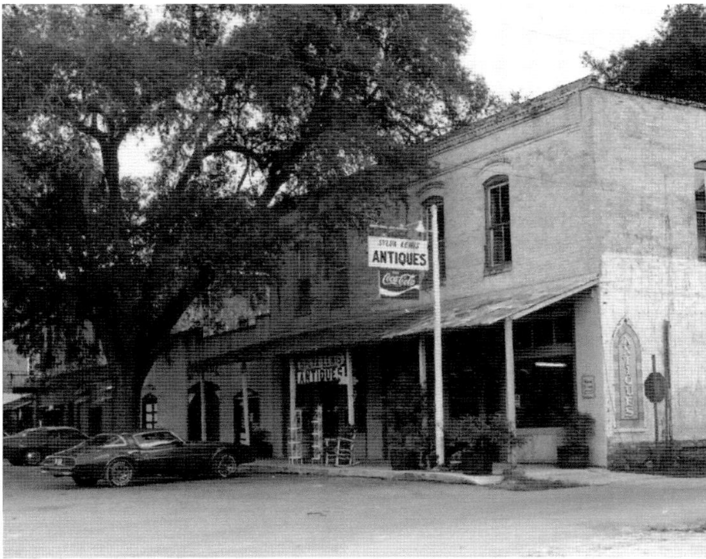

SYLVIA LEWIS'S ANTIQUE STORE

Micanopy is full of shops offering antiques, works of art and curios. Shown here is Sylvia Lewis's antique store from 1974. *Image courtesy of the Florida Photographic Collection.*

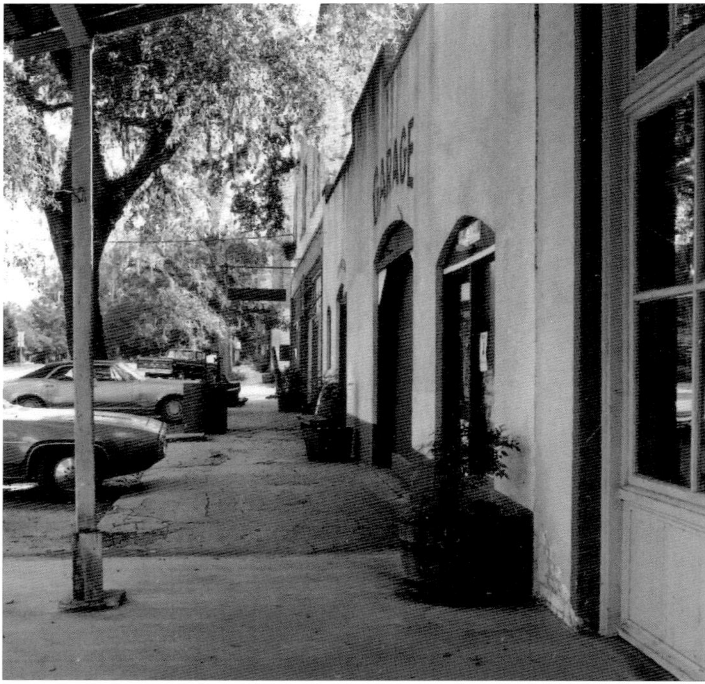

Mountain Garage

In 1913, John Mountain owned one of Micanopy's two cars and built this garage. Its operation was later taken over by his son, Buster. *Image courtesy of the Florida Photographic Collection.*

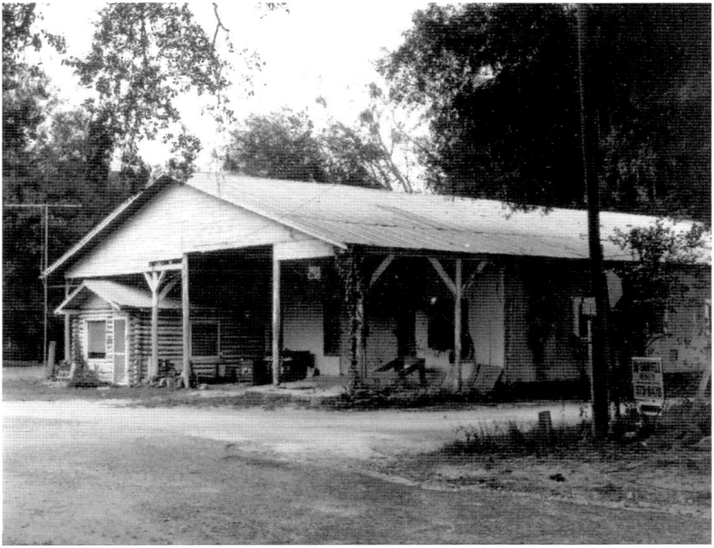

LOG CABIN

R.H. May built this log cabin in the 1920s for his wife, who ran the Log Cabin Café. It was built under this shelter used for grading and packing beans. *Image courtesy of the Florida Photographic Collection.*

Lodgings

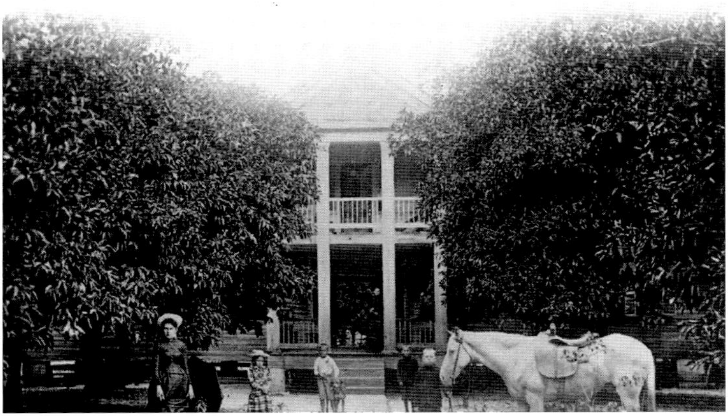

Bauknight House
This home was built before 1873 by Henry Bauknight. Later owner Adora Bauknight Smith is shown here in front of the porch with her five children. *Image courtesy of the Florida Photographic Collection.*

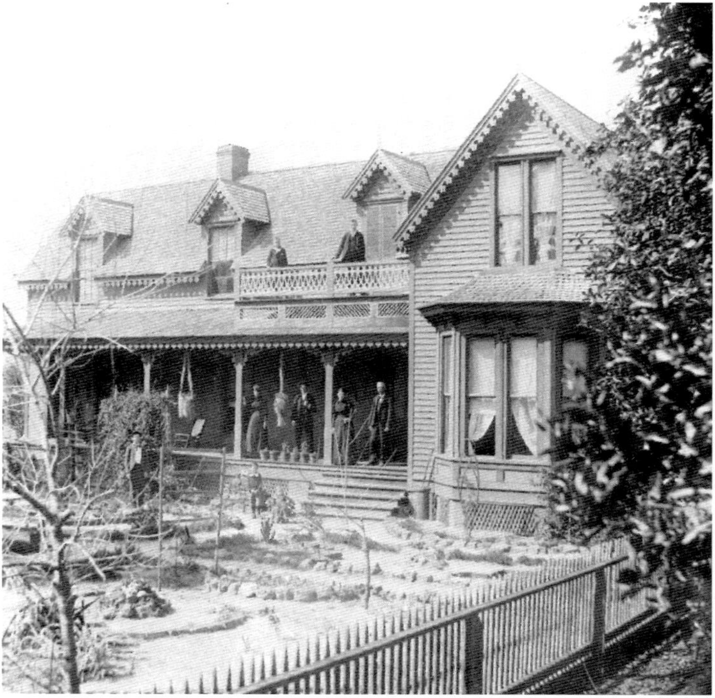

McCredie House

James McCredie built this home on Tuscawilla Road in 1871. In 1896, a year after this photo was taken, it burned and was rebuilt with the identical Victorian plan. *Image courtesy of the Florida Photographic Collection.*

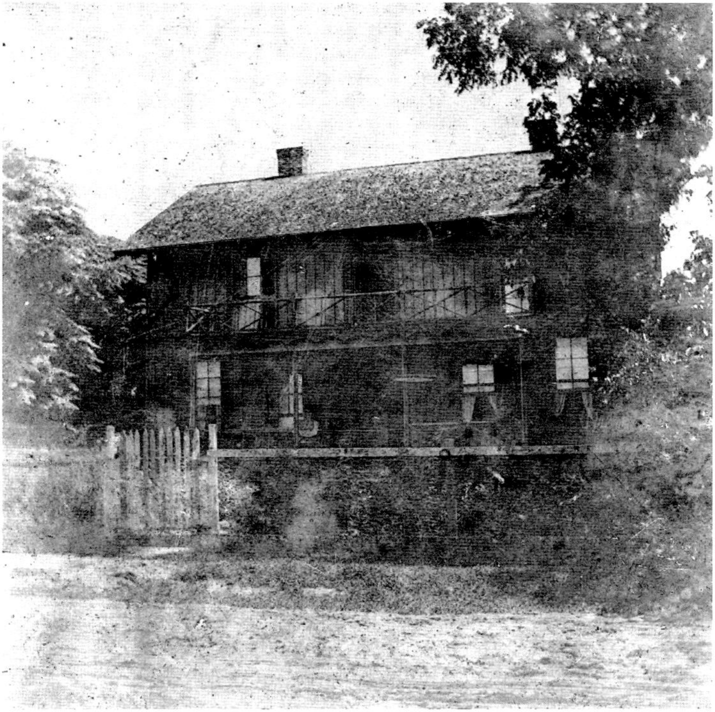

PARDEE HOME

This was the home of the Pardee family, constructed by 1893. It was located adjacent to the Pardee House Hotel and was torn down in 1971. *Image courtesy of the Florida Photographic Collection.*

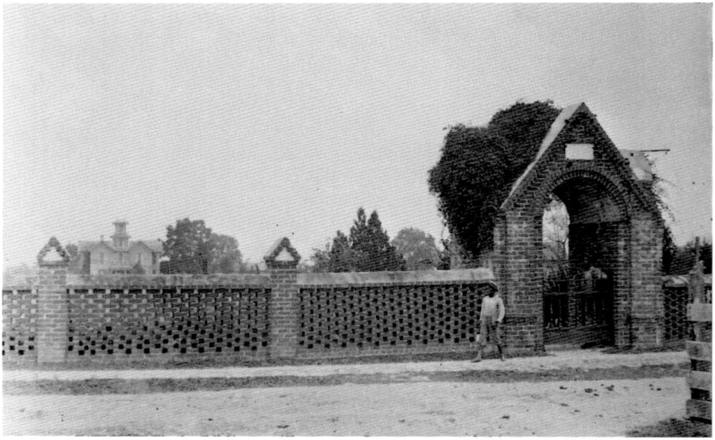

Montgomery House

Montgomery had three houses on the south side of Ocala Avenue that burned in 1895, 1911 and the 1930s. Across the street were his medical office and stable. *Image courtesy of the Florida Photographic Collection.*

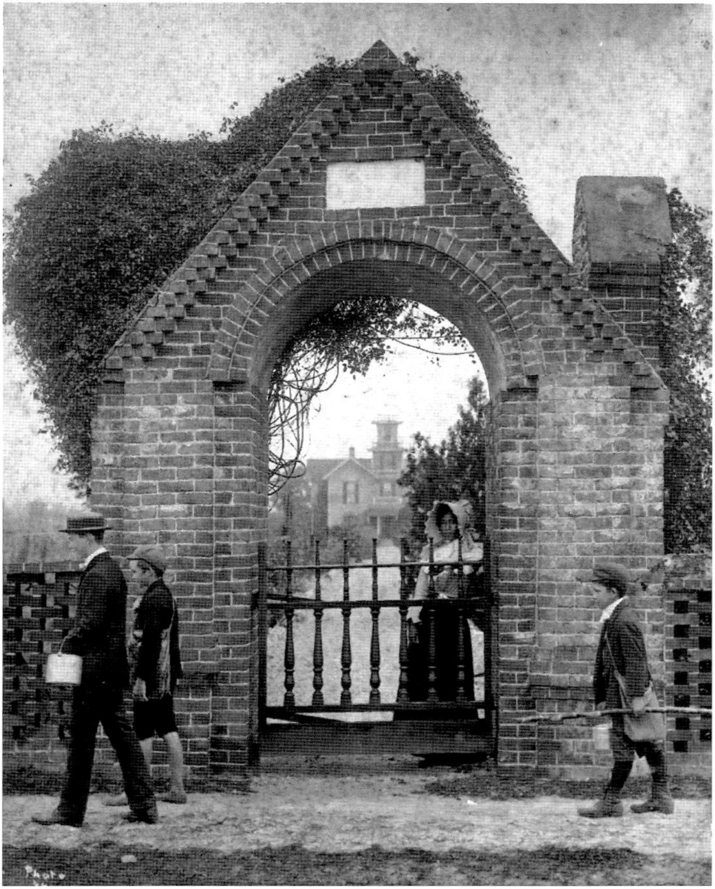

MONTGOMERY GATE

All that remains of the Lucius Montgomery estate is a portion of this wall and wrought-iron gate built in 1900 with bricks from the ballast of an English ship. *Image courtesy of the Florida Photographic Collection.*

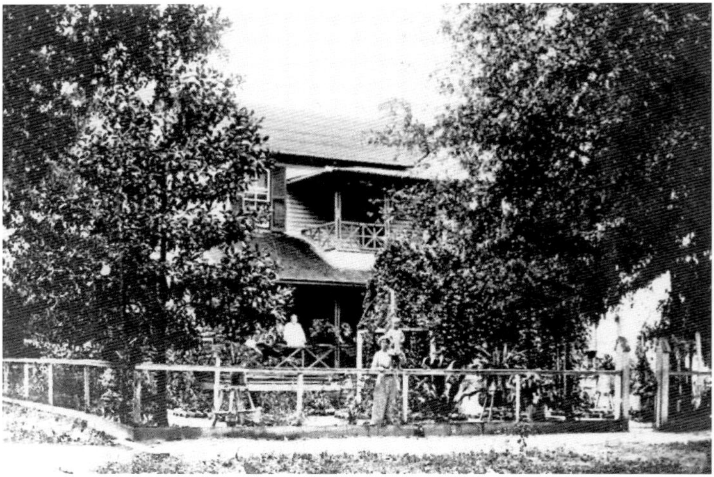

Chitty/Thrasher House

In 1900, Edward Chitty built this with two stories, and in 1917, John Thrasher bought it so he and his family could be close to their store. *Image courtesy of the Florida Photographic Collection.*

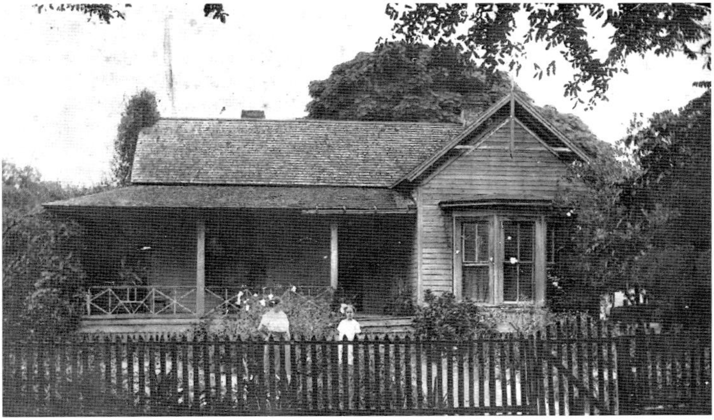

CARTER/MOTT/CHITTY HOUSE

This house on the west side of Division Street was built before 1900 by Mr. Carter. It was later owned by N.B. Mott and then Sam I. Chitty. *Image courtesy of the Florida Photographic Collection.*

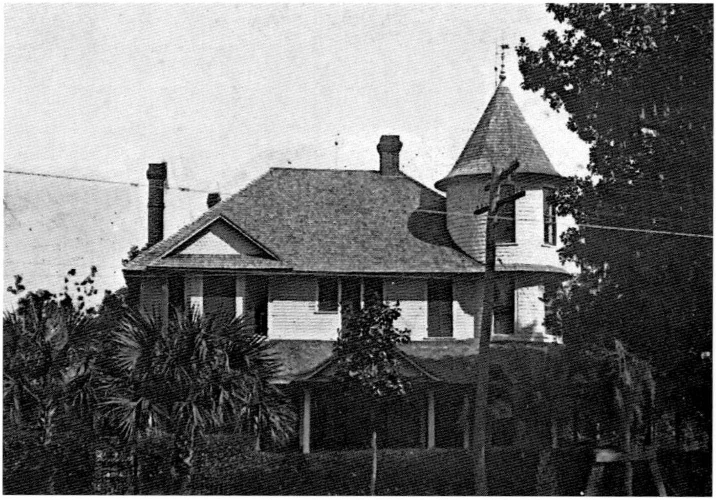

SIMONTON HOUSE

The original home on this corner faced south and was built by Dr. James Cooper. It was replaced in 1910 with the Simonton house shown here. *Image courtesy of the Florida Photographic Collection.*

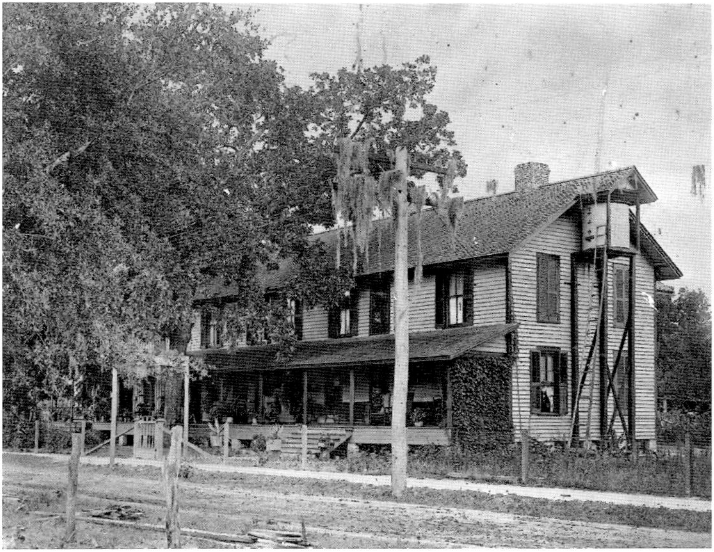

PARDEE HOUSE HOTEL
In 1901, W.B. Turner and his wife, Honoria Pardee, bought the Tuscawilla Hotel. After renovating it, they reopened it as the Pardee House Hotel. *Image courtesy of the Florida Photographic Collection.*

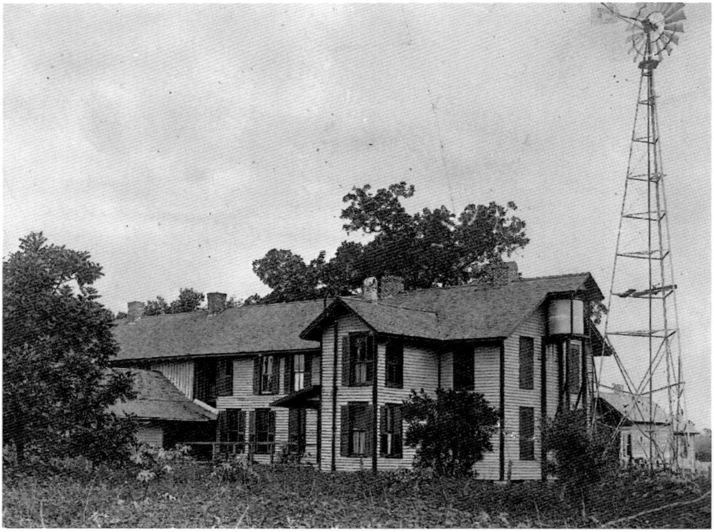

PARDEE HOUSE HOTEL

This is a rear view of the Pardee House, which was attached to the Pardee family residence. The hotel was converted to apartments and then was razed in 1971. *Image courtesy of the Florida Photographic Collection.*

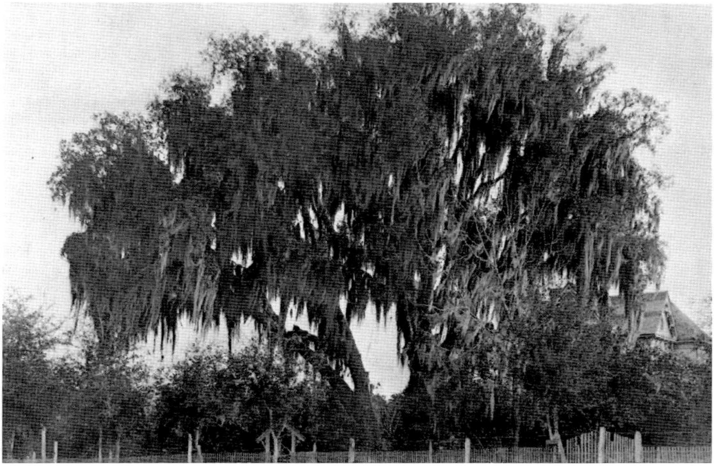

BARR HOUSE

The Barr house on Ocala Avenue is obscured by the huge twin oaks. They were damaged and cut back when the house burned in the 1920s. *Image courtesy of the Florida Photographic Collection.*

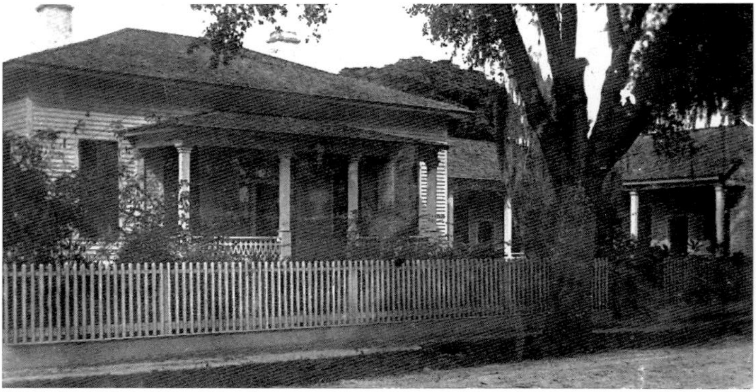

BOARDINGHOUSE

In the 1880s, this house on Seminary Street was the Winecoff Hotel. When this photo was taken in 1911, it was Mrs. Jesse Carter's boardinghouse. *Image courtesy of the Florida Photographic Collection.*

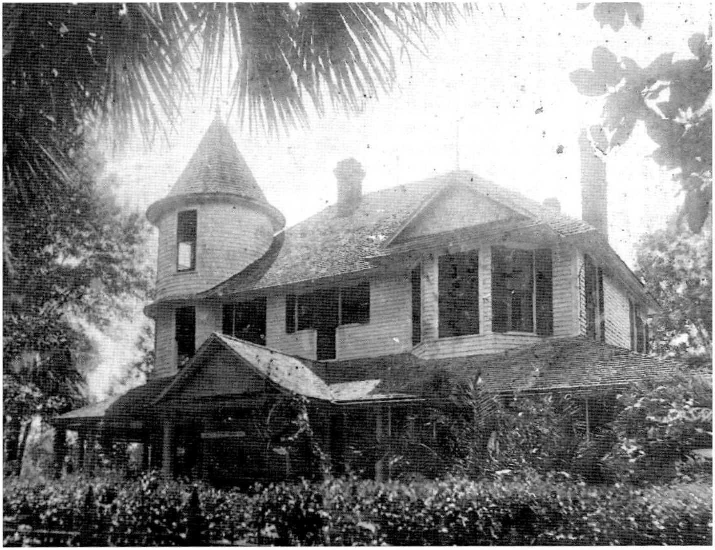

SIMONTON HOUSE
In 1910, merchant James Simonton built this Victorian-style home with Ionic columns and a porte-cochere. On his nearby ranch, Simonton raised cattle. *Image courtesy of the Florida Photographic Collection.*

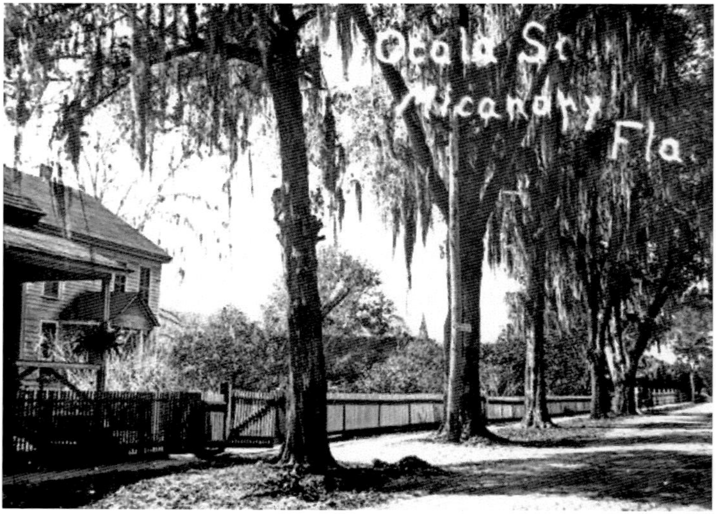

MEANS HOUSE

This is a 1914 view west along Ocala Street. To the left is the front porch of the home of Judge George W. and Mattie S. Means from South Carolina. *Image courtesy of the Florida Photographic Collection.*

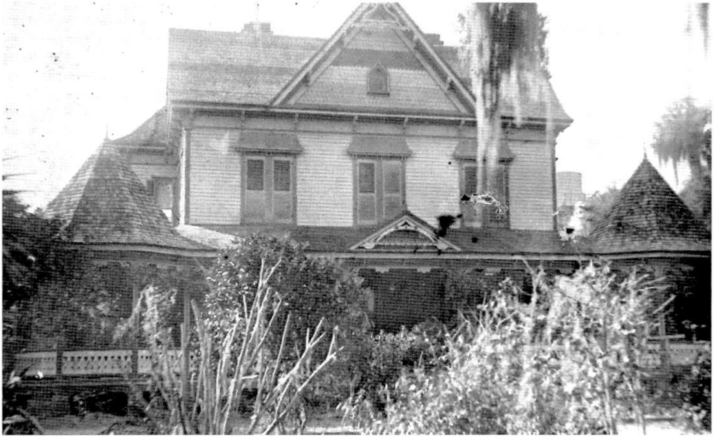

PAYNE HOUSE

Dr. George Payne arrived in Micanopy from Virginia in 1835 and was one of the area's first practicing physicians. He lived here in this imposing home. *Image courtesy of the Florida Photographic Collection.*

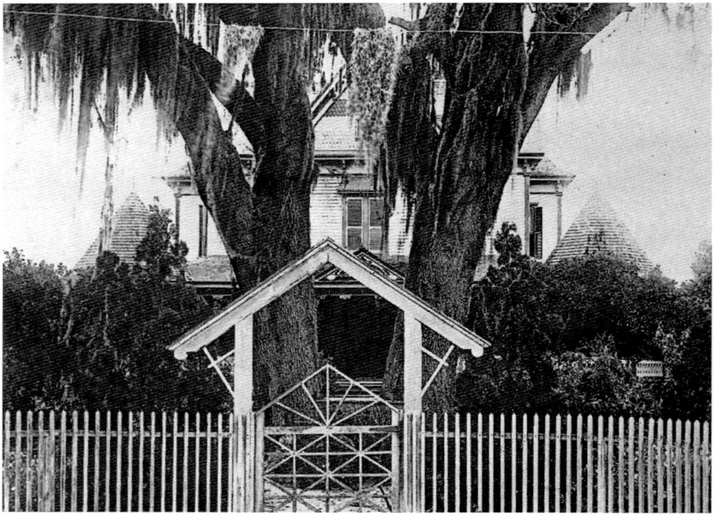

Payne Gate

In front of the Payne house on the south of Ocala Street was this intricate entrance gate and fence. Between it and the house are the twin Council Oaks. *Image courtesy of the Florida Photographic Collection.*

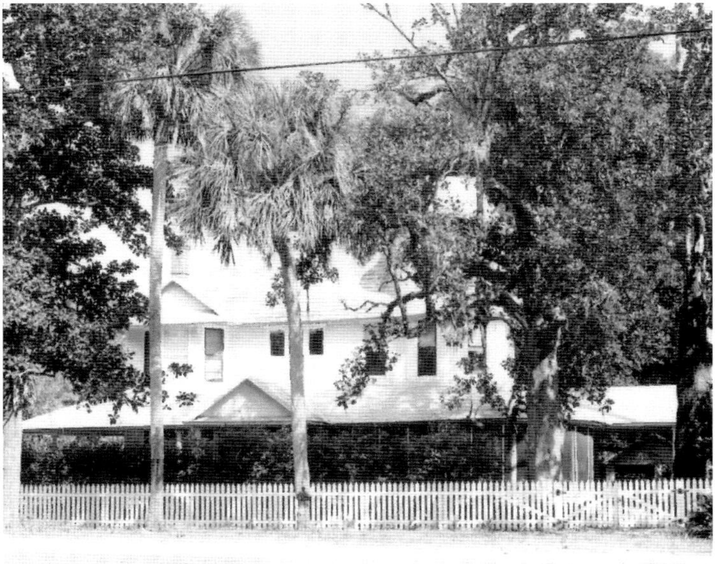

SIMONTON HOUSE
In 1911, the *Gainesville Sun* newspaper described this home of James Simonton as one of the prettiest houses in Micanopy. It still is. *Image courtesy of the Florida Photographic Collection.*

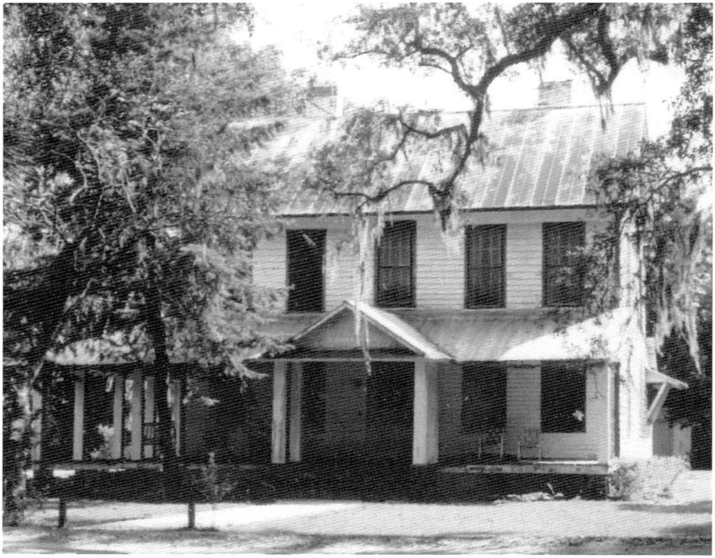

Stewart-Merry House

This home's two front rooms were part of a log office built by Dr. James A. Stewart in 1855. It is the oldest known house in town. *Image courtesy of the Florida Photographic Collection.*

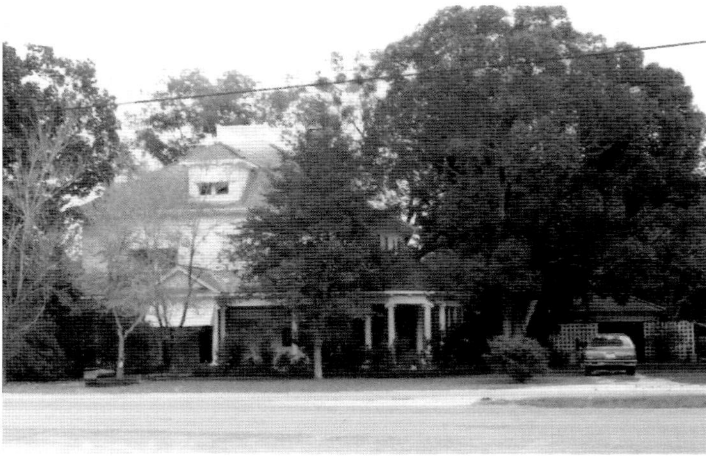

FONTAINE HOUSE
This is the second home on this lot for Benjamin Fontaine, built after his first burned in 1911. He ran a general store across Cholokka Boulevard. *Image courtesy of the Florida Photographic Collection.*

In-Town Scenes

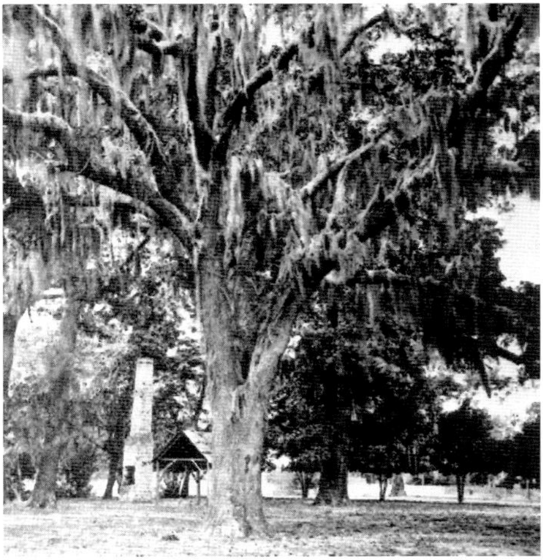

COUNCIL OAK

This is an 1875 view of a site where Chief Micanopy may have sat in council in the 1830s. It is half of a pair of oaks adjacent to George Payne's home. *Image courtesy of the Florida Photographic Collection.*

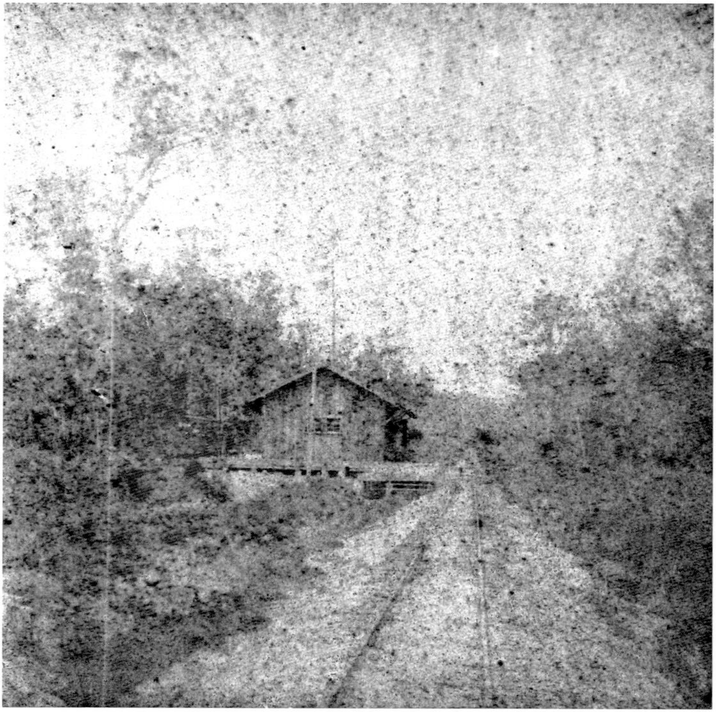

Railroad Depot

A 3.6-mile branch line of the Florida Southern Railway ran to this depot on Okehumpkee Street. It mostly carried freight, and it went out of service in 1945. *Image courtesy of the Florida Photographic Collection.*

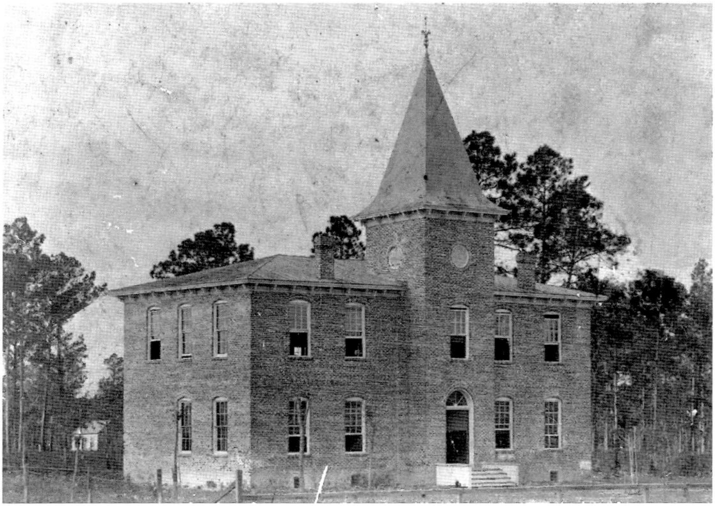

SCHOOL

First known as the Lamisophonian Institute, this school was built in 1895 and was enlarged in 1912 and 1923. It later was Micanopy Junior High School. *Image courtesy of the Florida Photographic Collection.*

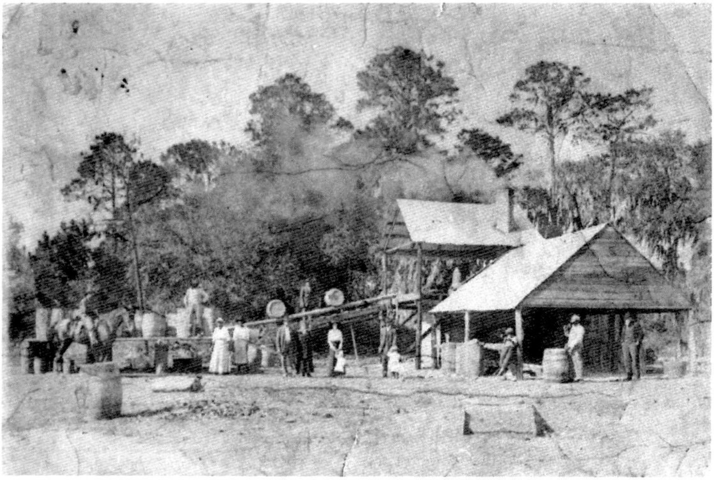

Turpentine Still

The couple holding the children by this turpentine still is Mr. and Mrs. R.T. Crouch. The other couple is John and Maude Roberts. *Image courtesy of the Florida Photographic Collection.*

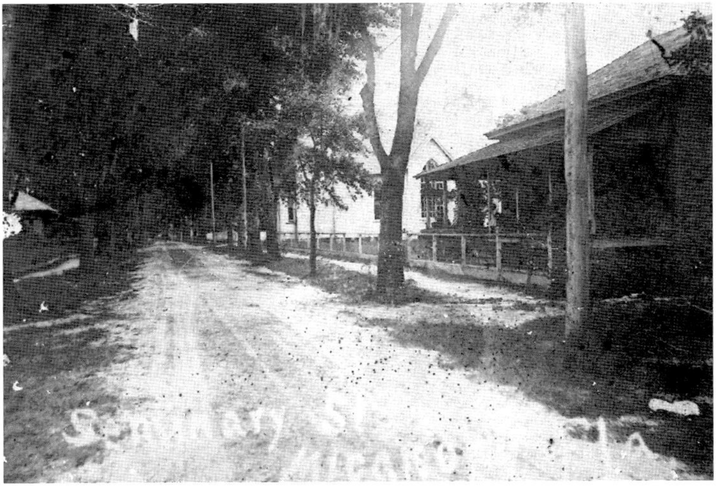

SEMINARY AVENUE
This street was named for the East Florida Seminary, whose wooden building was erected on it in 1852. The seminary closed in 1860, when the teacher joined the army. *Image courtesy of the Florida Photographic Collection.*

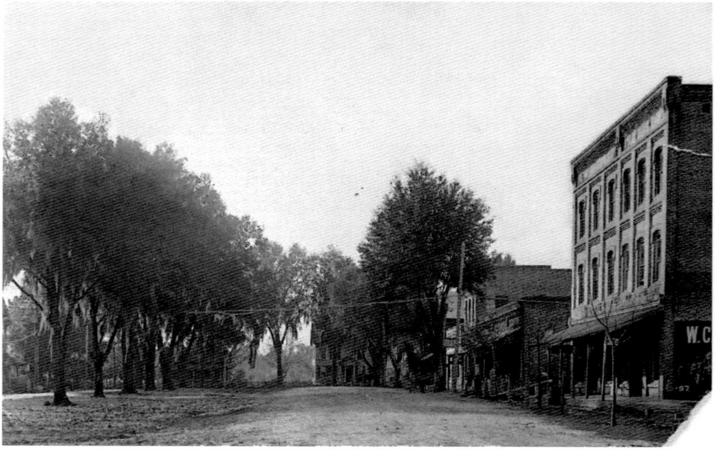

Cholokka Boulevard

This is looking south on Cholokka Boulevard in 1909. The three closest structures from right to left are the Feaster Building, the Benjamin Building and the bank. *Image courtesy of the Florida Photographic Collection.*

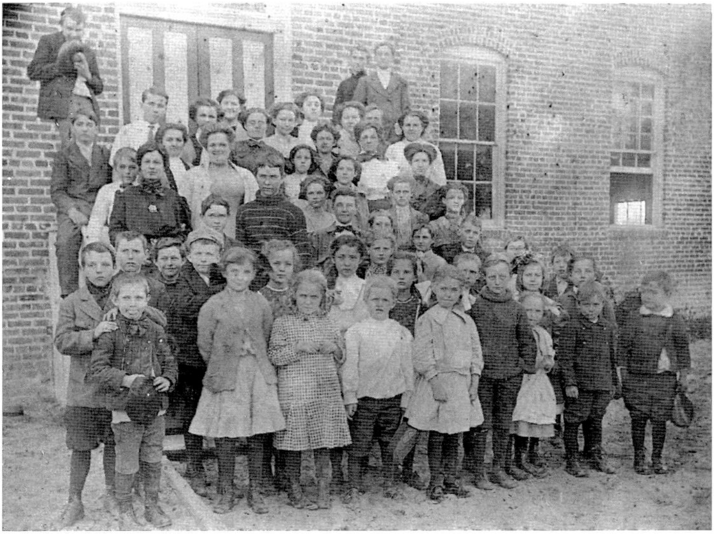

Elementary School Students
This is the 1909 class photo of the elementary school students of Micanopy. The building was officially designated as Alachua County School No. 15. *Image courtesy of the Florida Photographic Collection.*

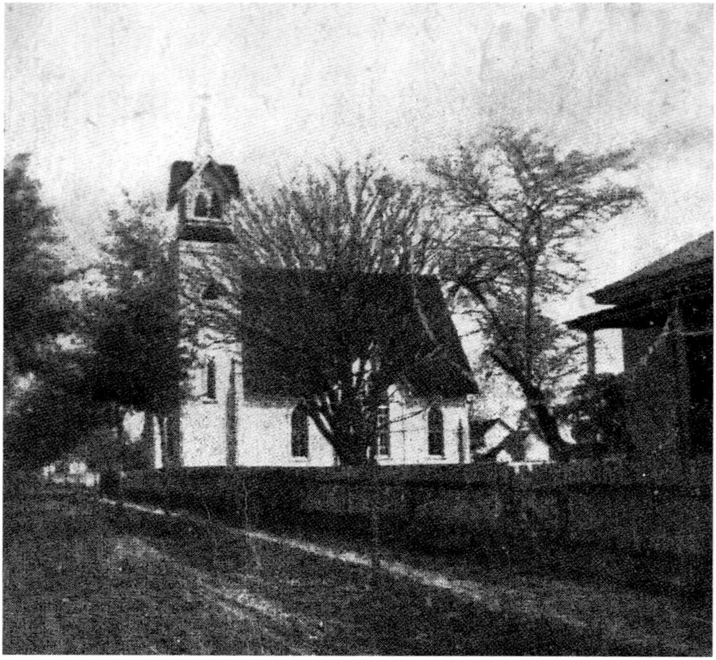

MICANOPY METHODIST CHURCH

Built in 1892, this Gothic church replaced an 1859 sanctuary. When a spark from a burning house crossed Seminary Avenue in 1933, this one burned down. *Image courtesy of the Florida Photographic Collection.*

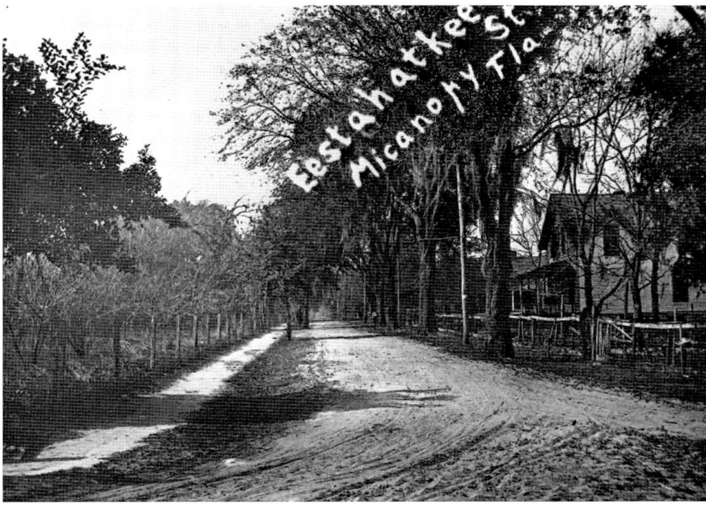

ESTAUALLKEE STREET

This street looked like this in 1912. It is now paved, the large house is gone and the Ward Chapel AME Church replaced a portion of the grove on the left. *Image courtesy of the Florida Photographic Collection.*

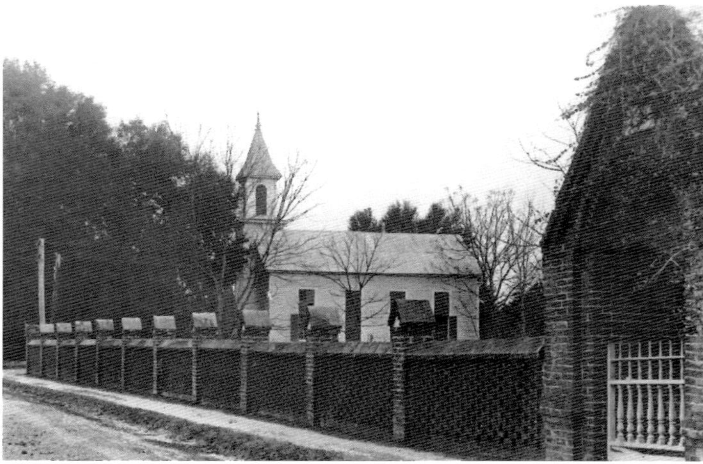

Baptist Church

This Micanopy Baptist Church was built in the 1880s, and in the 1960s, it was replaced by another Baptist church elsewhere. This one was turned into a residence. *Image courtesy of the Florida Photographic Collection.*

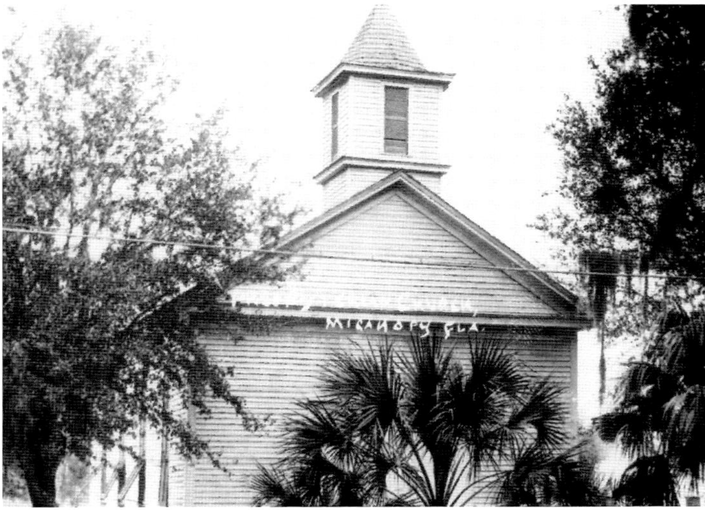

PRESBYTERIAN/EPISCOPAL CHURCH
This 1870 church still stands, but its use has changed. It began as a Presbyterian church and became the Episcopal Church of the Mediator in 1987. *Image courtesy of the Florida Photographic Collection.*

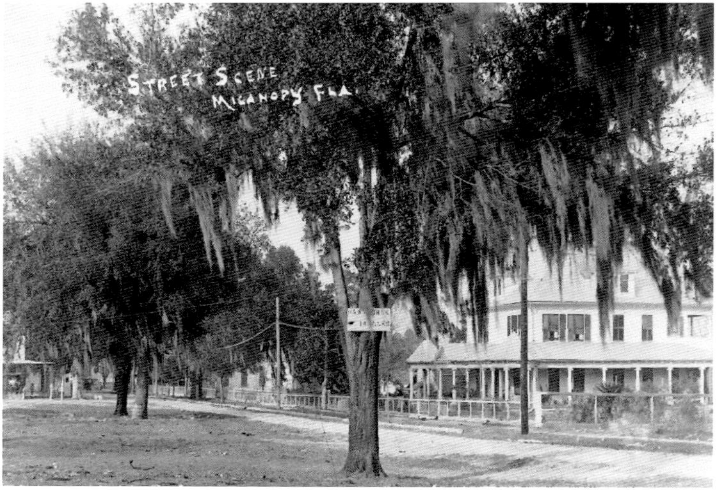

CHOLOKKA BOULEVARD

Looking north in 1915 are seen the Tampa and Jacksonville (T&J) Railroad depot on the left, the large home of Benjamin Fontaine and the Presbyterian church in between. *Image courtesy of the Florida Photographic Collection.*

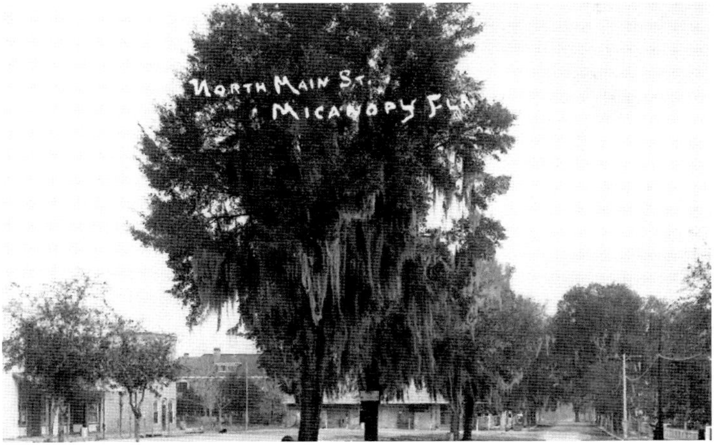

RAILROAD DEPOT

The building in the middle was constructed in 1895 for the Gainesville and Gulf Railroad. It later was known as the T&J Railroad. *Image courtesy of the Florida Photographic Collection.*

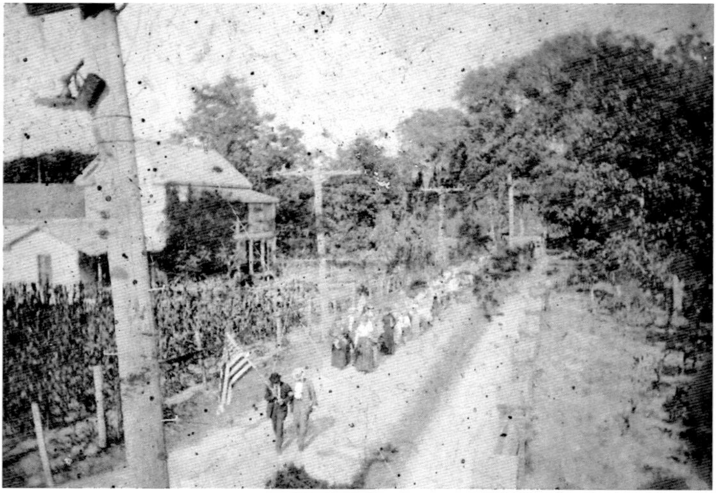

MEMORIAL DAY PARADE

The 1918 Memorial Day parade heads west along Smith Street, passing the brick wall of Dr. Lucius Montgomery, toward the Micanopy Cemetery. *Image courtesy of the Florida Photographic Collection.*

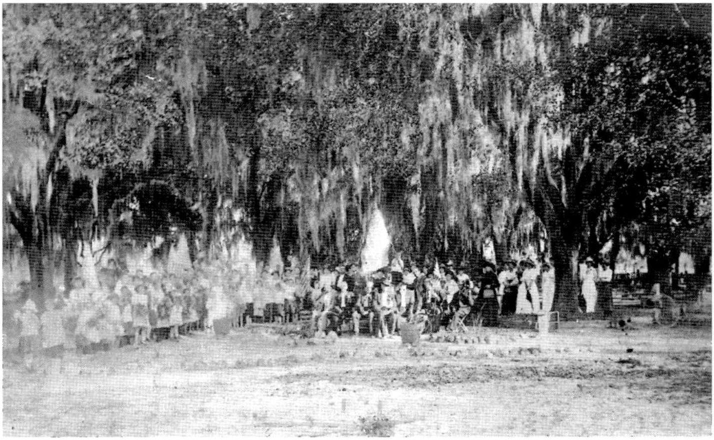

MEMORIAL DAY CEREMONY

The parade ended at the cemetery, which was founded in 1826. Wreaths were laid on the older graves, while veterans sat and remembered. *Image courtesy of the Florida Photographic Collection.*

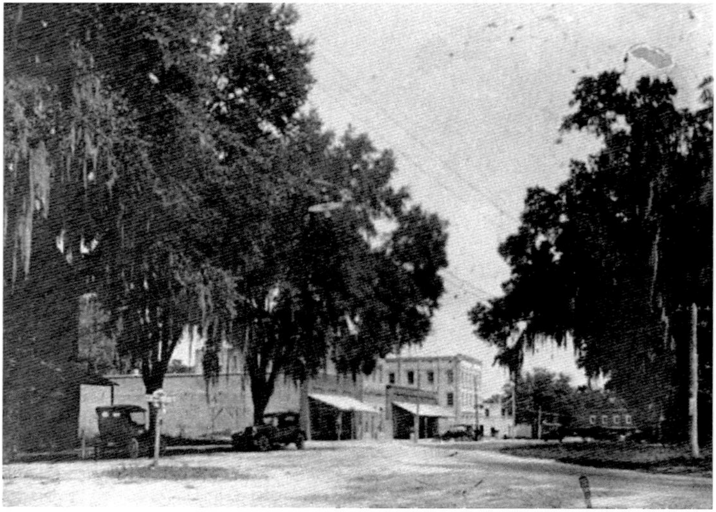

Cholokka Boulevard

On the right in this 1920 photo is the town square. It is believed that it was where Edward Wanton set up his trading post in 1821. *Image courtesy of the Florida Photographic Collection.*

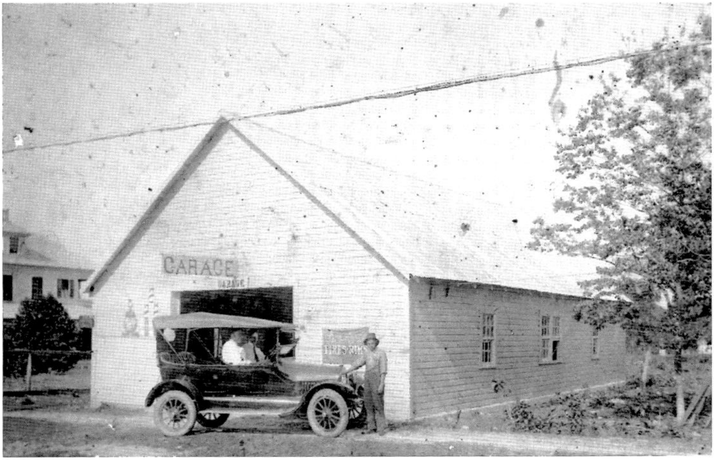

GARAGE

This large automobile repair shop was located on Cholokka Boulevard when this photo was taken in 1920. It later burned down. *Image courtesy of the Florida Photographic Collection.*

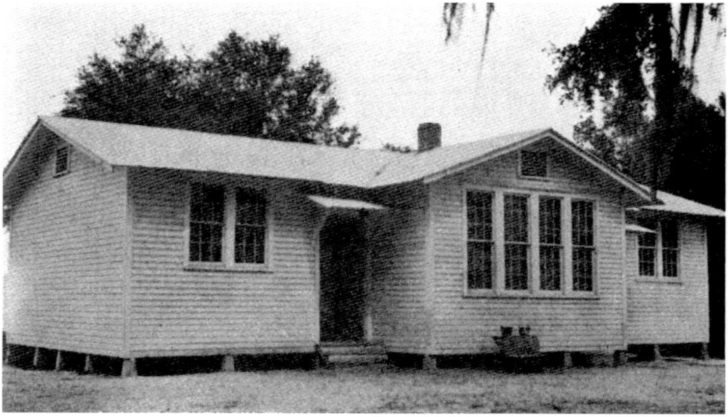

Rosenwald School

Shown here in 1930 is Micanopy's wooden school for black children. It, and more than five thousand other schools, was built with funds donated by clothier Julius Rosenwald. *Image courtesy of the Florida Photographic Collection.*

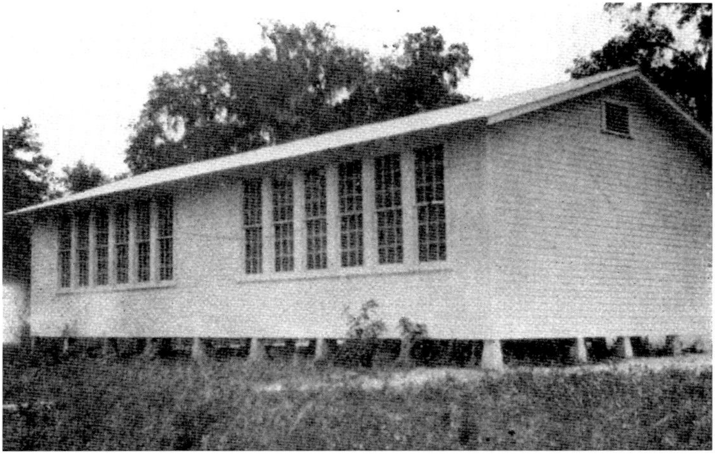

ROSENWALD SCHOOL

This is another view of the school paid for by a donation from a principal of Sears, Roebuck and Company. His foundation donated over $4 million for Southern schools. *Image courtesy of the Florida Photographic Collection.*

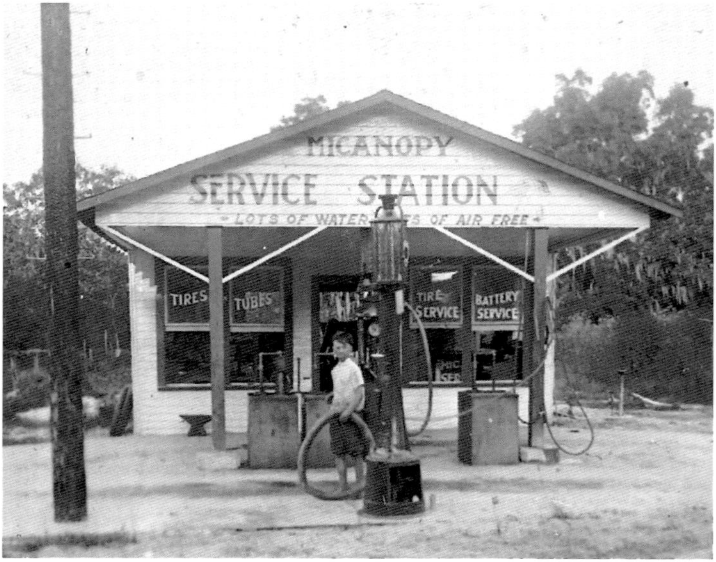

Micanopy Service Station

This modern (for its time) service station with a gas pump was built and owned by Jesse C. Rowell. It replaced an earlier one on the site that had burned. *Image courtesy of the Florida Photographic Collection.*

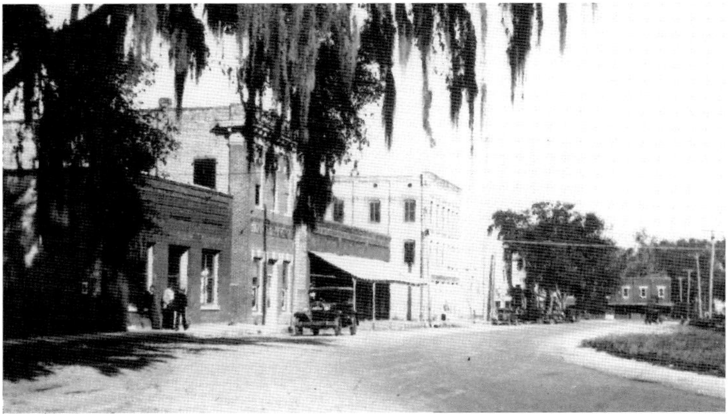

Cholokka Boulevard

Looking north in 1934, the first brick building on the left was a store. It was replaced by the Sherouse Garage and then a wooden antique store. *Image courtesy of the Florida Photographic Collection.*

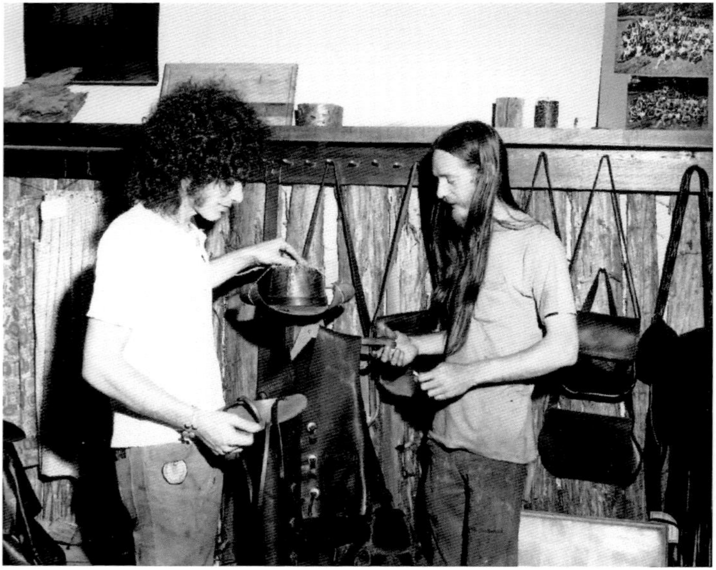

ARTS AND CRAFTS

Micanopy has for many years been a Mecca for artists and craftsmen. Painters, potters, leather workers and many others display their works in local galleries and shops. *Image courtesy of the Florida Photographic Collection.*

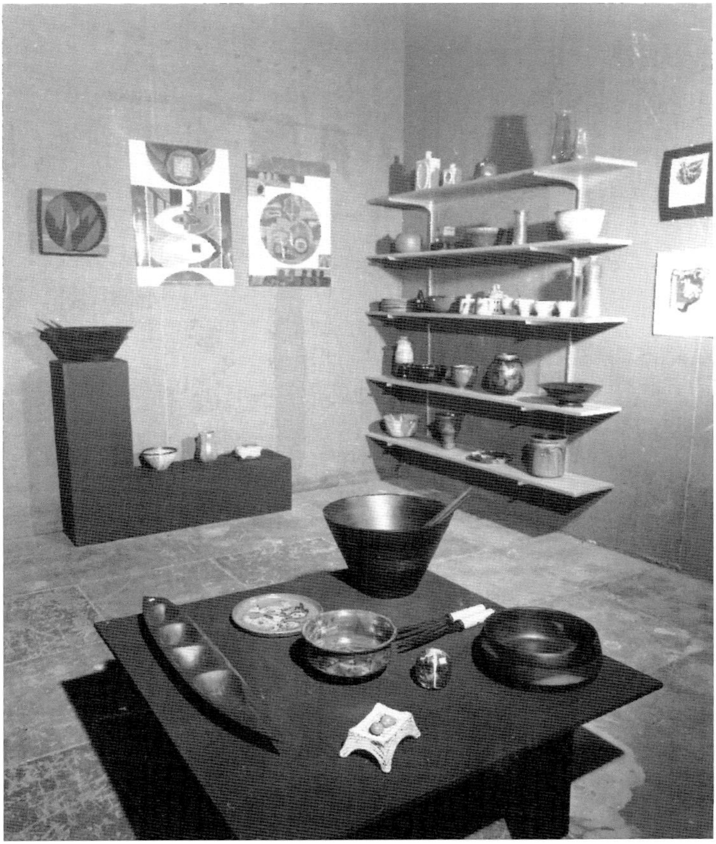

ARTS AND CRAFTS

In the mid-1970s, the annual Fall Harvest Festival was founded. Continuing today, it attracts artists and craftsmen and visitors from Florida and elsewhere. *Image courtesy of the Florida Photographic Collection.*

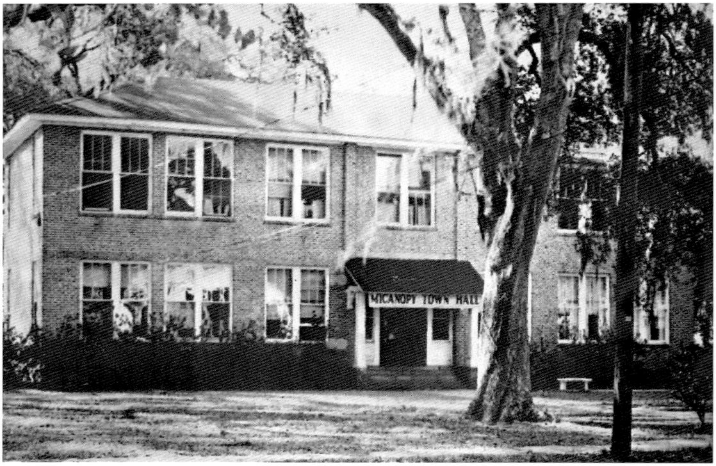

TOWN HALL

In 1973, the 1895 brick building that had been the Micanopy public school was transformed into the town hall. It also houses the library. *Image courtesy of the Florida Photographic Collection.*

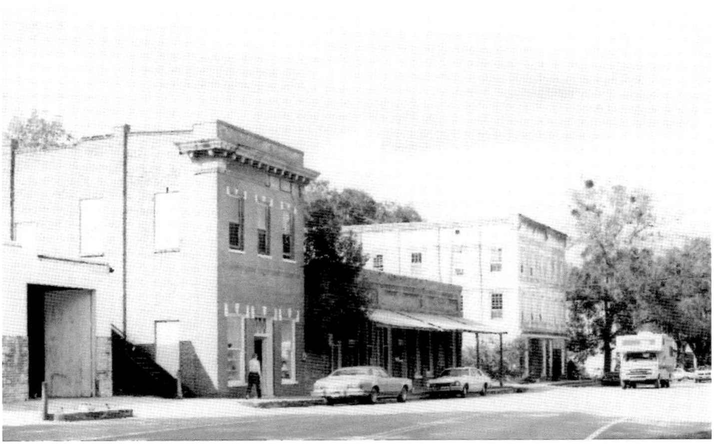

CHOLOKKA BOULEVARD

Looking north on Cholokka Boulevard, the building on the left with the large open door is the former Sherouse Garage. Remnants of gas pumps are visible out front. *Image courtesy of the Florida Photographic Collection.*

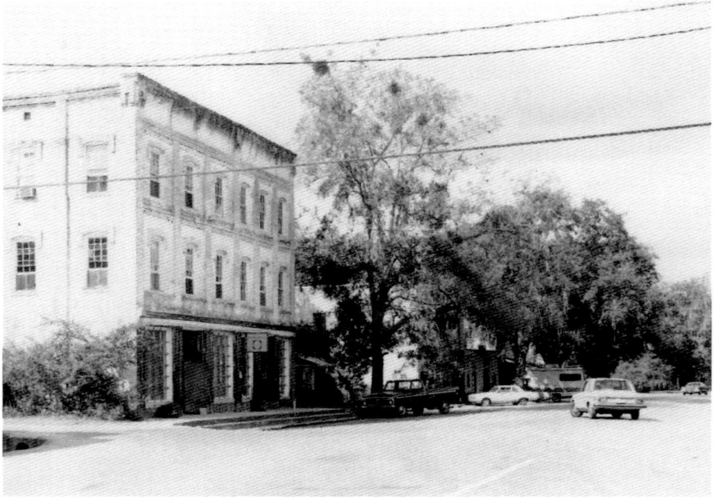

CHOLOKKA BOULEVARD

In 1983, most of Micanopy, the oldest Florida town not on a waterway, was added to the National Register of Historic Places. The historic district includes buildings along this street. *Image courtesy of the Florida Photographic Collection.*

Bibliography

Anderson, Lars. *Paynes Prairie: The Great Savanna: A History and Guide*. Sarasota, FL: Pineapple Press, Inc., 2001.

Davis, Jess G. *History of Alachua County 1824–1969*. Gainesville, FL: Alachua County Historical Commission, 1969.

Opdyke, John B., ed. *Alachua County: A Sesquicentennial Tribute*. Gainesville, FL: Alachua County Historical Commission, 1974.

Watkins, Caroline B. *The Story of Historic Micanopy*. Gainesville, FL: Alachua County Historical Commission, 1976.

Webber, Carl. *The Eden of the South*. Micanopy, FL: Micanopy Publishing Co., 1995. Reprint of 1883 material.

About the Author

Steve Rajtar grew up near Cleveland, Ohio, came to Florida to go to college, earned degrees in mathematics, anthropology, law and taxation and decided to stay. He has been involved with the Boy Scouts for thirty years and is an activity leader with the Florida Trail Association. The combination of a love for the outdoors and local history has resulted in his establishment of over 150 historical tour routes through the communities of central Florida. These routes can be used by anyone to get up close and personal with the region's historic sites. He has written several books on various aspects of hiking and history and loves to guide tours by foot, bicycle and kayak.